# Dedication

This book is dedicated to my mother, a woman possessed of infinite patience, unlimited wisdom, and unending encouragement. I write today, because she told me I could when we first met.

# Table of Contents

**Acknowledgments**      **xiii**

**Prologue**      **xv**

**Chapter 1**    **Why Telecommuting Is an Idea Whose Time Has Come**    **3**

What Is Telecommuting?    3

Why Now?    4

Who's Using Telecommuting Now?   8

How Telecommuting
     Increases Productivity    10

Eliminating Unnecessary
     Expenses    13

Hiring the Handicapped    14

Increasing the Pool                                    15

Environmental Impact                              16

Preparation for Natural Disasters  17

Employee Benefits from
    Telecommuting                                   18

Increased Productivity                          18

The Cost of Going to Work              20

Tangible Savings Relating to
    Employment                                       20

Other Factors Impact the
    Corporate Employee                       22

Benefits which Both Labor and
    Management  Share                          24

Reduced Pollution                               24

Mass Transit                                        25

Security as a Factor in the
    Metropolitan Environment           26

Reduced Dependence on Foreign
    Petroleum                                          27

Social and Personal
    Situational Benefits                        28


Chapter 2       **Finding the Right Personnel and
Project to Implement a
Telecommuting Program         31**

Profiles of a Telecommuter and
    the Problems Attendant to
    the Program                                      31

*Self-Starters*                                          32

*Job Experience*                                         32

*Communication Skills*                                   33

*Organization as a Way of Life*                          35

*Organizing the Home Office*                             36

*Establishing a Schedule*                                37

*Becoming Comfortable in the
    New Environment*                                     38

*Establishing a Regimen*                                 40

*Adapting Others to the
    Telecommuter's Environment*                          41

*Managing the Manager*                                   44

*Profile of the Telecommuting
    Manager*                                             45

*Communicating the Expectations
    of the Job to the
    Telecommuter*                                        47


**Chapter 3**    **How to Begin a
                   Telecommuting Program**               **53**

Implementation of a
Telecommuting Program                                    53

*Planning the Move*                                      54

*Implementation of the Plan*                             59

The Three Major Factors of a
    Telecommuting Project                                61

**Chapter 4**    **Managing, Monitoring, and**
            **Motivating the New**
            **Telecommuter**                    **65**

            How to Manage the
                Telecommuter                 65

            *Assignment of Production*          66

            *Establish Goals and Timetables*    67

            *Timetables*                        68

            *Timeframes*                        70

            *Timelines*                         71

            Preparing the Telecommuter       72

            *Change in Working Hours*          72

            Compensation and Benefits        74

            Coming Back to the Fold          75

            The Contract                     76


**Chapter 5**    **Guides for Setting Successful**
            **Parameters for Telecommuters 81**

            Eight Guidelines Toward the
                Making of a Great
                Telecommuter Manager          81

            Time as a Factor in Setting Up a
                Telecommuting Program        86

            The Plan                         87

            Recruitment Procedures           89

            Implementation                   92

**Chapter 6**    **Addressing the Various Factors of Liability Inherent in Telecommuting**    **99**

Liabilities Involved in Telecommuting    99

*Product Liability*    99

*Employee Liability*    100

*Property Liability*    102

*Tax Liabilities*    104

*Security Liability*    109

**Chapter 7**    **Telecommuting as It Applies to Government and Semi-Public Entities**    **119**

San Diego County Telecommuting Program    119

*Setting Up the Program*    122

*The Screening Process*    123

*The Employee Characteristic Assessment*    123

*The Telecommuter Screening Survey*    127

*Supervisor Screening Survey*    127

*The Pre-Pilot Attitudinal Survey*    132

*Management's Survey*    132

*Telecommuting Survey for Employees*    136

*The Results of the County of
San Diego Telecommuting
Pilot Project*                    142

*Ambassador College and the
SwifNet Project*                  143

**Chapter 8    A Study of Telecommuting
as It Applies to Private
Corporations                      149**

Crane and Associates              149

California Western Life—
Worst Case Scenario           151

The Travelers Group—
A Study in Perfection         155

Megatek Industries                158

**Chapter 9    Telecommuting as a Means of
Legislative Compliance        165**

*Federal Statutes Concerning
Telecommuting*                166

*The United States Tax Code as
an Instrument of Change*      168

*Support from the President
of the United States*         169

Organized Labor and Its
Position in Regard to
Telecommuting                 170

**Chapter 10**　　**The Global Implications of Telecommuting as It Relates to the 21st Century**　　**179**

Telecommuting as It Relates to a Global Economy　　179

Five Factors Most Responsible for the Increased Competition in the World Economy　　182

Service Industries in the United States by the Year 1993　　185

Telecommuting Experiments in Europe　　189

*The Netherlands*　　189

**Epilogue**　　**195**

**Glossary of Terms**　　**197**

**Index**　　**201**

# Acknowledgments

I would like to acknowledge the contributions of the following individuals and corporations, without whose help, this book could not have been written.

AFL/CIO
Ambassador College
David H. Autor
Steve Belikoff
Bruce Berend
Beau Boulter
David H. Bunell
William M. Butler
Crain and Associates
Dennis Chamot
Peggy Connerton
County of San Diego
Susan Cowell
Joseph J. Davis

Phylis Glasheen
John Holtzclaw
International Ladies Garment Workers
Donald H. Ledbetter
Loral-Conic Corporation
Jane MacCarthy
Rodrick MacKenzie
David E. Mahfood
Sebastian P. Mahfood
Megateck Corporation
Pacific Bell
Janet Reincke
Rob Reincke
Ed Risse
Linda T. Risse
Synergy Planning Corporation
Service Employees Union
Diane Song
Antonia B. Stone
Travelers Insurance

# Prologue

New roads and new bridges are being built each and every day, special highways made out of fine strands of copper wire. They are the roads by which the corporate businesses of America will transport their most important commodity: information! They require no public tax money, cause no tie-ups in traffic, and best of all, increase the productivity of both the company and the worker. The results of these new highways are still being analyzed, but one thing is certain: once Americans begin to travel these roads, the older, more traditional routes to work will be abandoned and discarded by all but the most pedestrian of workers. The new super highway is called *telecommuting*, and it seems like something straight out of a Jules Verne novel!

Henry Ford revolutionized the concept of mass production when he perfected the assembly line.

Move the work to the worker and watch him do a faster, more efficient job. Ford was right then, and telecommuters are right now. The single greatest waste of American resources occurs daily between the hours of seven to nine each morning and five to seven each evening. Each working day during those four hours, corporate employees waste time, money, fuel, and perhaps the most important of all, their best creative energies trying to get from their homes to their offices and back home again. When they arrive at their destinations, their nerves are shot and they already feel as if they've put in an additional hour or two at work—hours for which they'll not be paid.

America cannot continue to build more and wider highways, construct more and taller office buildings, create more and bigger parking lots, and waste more and scarcer fuels in a constant stream of increased business activity. Somewhere this madness must stop! Our skies are polluted beyond endurance, our highways are clogged to the point that a worker can spend almost as much time getting to and from work as he does once he's there, and parking spaces are becoming things to die for. The answer is not found in scaled down businesses, nor is it found in moving corporate headquarters to the boonies. The answer is as close as the phone on your desk. The answer is telecommuting.

Telecommuting is the official buzzword for the simple concept of having a worker work where he is the most productive. It is a simple concept! Look around a typical office. There are desks, chairs, and rooms. There are spaces where employees sit in cubicles and perform tasks for which they are regularly compensated. There are computers, fax machines, telephones, and other modern office equipment. There may be special rooms for conferences and meetings between different levels of management; there may be rooms allocated for breaks and for socializing between working hours. There may be an area where workers may smoke, drink coffee, or eat lunch. Outside this brick and glass construction, you will often find a huge area (usually larger than a football field) reserved for parking.

Connected to the buildings, either by underground installations or overhead wires, are millions of feet of cable: some are used to conduct electricity and some to connect the phone systems to another building across the street or across the world. This is a typical office complex. On any given work day, it virtually throbs with the combined heartbeat of thousands of workers—all hurrying to perform the tasks for which they are employed, all scurrying about, looking busy, acting busy, and all concerned with how they look and how their work is perceived by their superiors. They compete with each other for the next promotion—for the next level of employment. They cast their eyes upward toward the crystal palace on the top floor to the executive washrooms (admittance by invitation only).

These workers are concerned about the jobs they do and their level of production. Their managers judge them by how quickly they achieve their objectives, by how productive they appear to be. They watch and weigh the output of each employee. Those who produce the most, accomplish the greatest amount of their quota, will, in a fair world, get promoted. Those who do less than expected will not. In some cases, where management exhibits a high degree of discernment, those who lag behind will eventually be sent home, their services no longer needed by the corporation.

All this is as it should be. However, the compelling factor is that the only element that accomplishes any work—the only entity which allows the corporation to prosper or forces it to die—is not the brick and glass structure, nor the parking lot, the security force, the supersonic elevator, the computer, the fax machine, the calculator, or the telephone and copy machine. It is, quite obviously, the worker! The worker is what produces production! The most technologically advanced work stations in the world cannot sell a widget, cannot create and implement their own programs, and cannot set goals and objectives. Only managers and their workers can do that.

People! Employees doing the jobs they are paid to do, doing them with the expertise their managers expect of them, are the backbone of American business. Telecommuting will make America more productive and will ultimately make America more profitable. The bottom line of every enterprise in a free-market economy is to turn a profit. Telecommuting offers corporate America the opportunity to do just that.

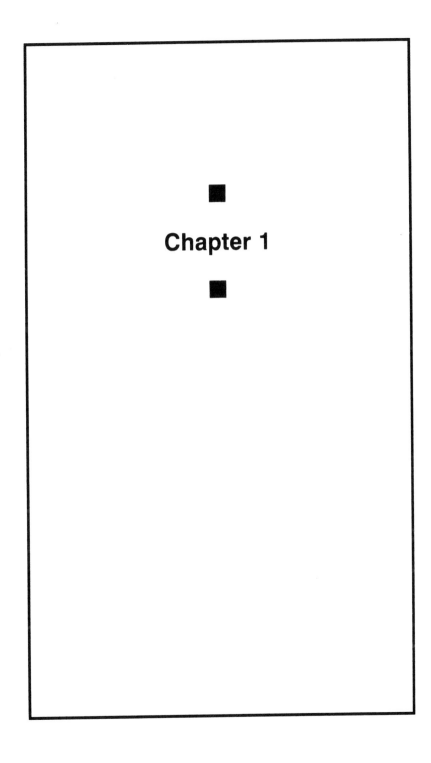

# Chapter 1

# Why Telecommuting Is an Idea Whose Time Has Come

## **W**hat Is Telecommuting?

Telecommuting breaks down into three distinct categories. Since its inception in 1972, it has evolved from strictly a method of moving the work to the worker, into a full blown concept encompassing those who work at home, either full or part time, those who work in a satellite office, and those who work at neighborhood work centers.

In the last several years, however, most research concerning telecommuting has centered around the concept of the corporate employee who performs his or her job primarily from an office in his or her home. Non-traditional approaches to corporate life take time to find their stroke within individual corporations. So it is with telecommuting. There are as many different approaches to telecommuting as there are types of telecommuters. Telecommuting is as much a matter of style as it is utility.

# **W**hy Now?

Before we can study how telecommuting could work for your company, an understanding of how telecommuting came to be will prove useful. The first question to be addressed is "Why now?"

Business is business. Calvin Coolidge said it best when he said, "The business of America is business." As a world leader in so many aspects of business, America brought the concept of free-enterprise to a fine art. What started as a national mish-mash of farmers, cottage industries, and shippers soon grew into the largest industrial complex the world had ever seen. Harnessing and managing that creative energy in such a manner as to yield maximum profits from minimum investments soon became the conscious effort of every businessman in America. It was no sooner than the mom and pop operations grew into viable companies that these companies then found themselves up to their necks in competition with similar organizations. Soon it became a battle for survival. If there were fifty companies manufacturing widgets, they would compete with each other, cutting prices, cutting costs, until only a handful survived. Those that did survive did so by maximizing every tool at their disposal. More often than not, that tool was sharper management.

But despite this rush to competition, one thing stayed pretty much the same: THE HOME OFFICE! From 1900 until 1960, not much changed in the way business was conducted. Heavy wooden roll-top desks gave way to heavy, grey metal desks, which in time gave way to light, wooden desks. The office messenger boy gave way to the telephone. The office mail delivery gave way to voice mail or E-Mail. The hand cranked adding machine yielded its spot to the calculator. Even the old Underwood manual typewriter surrendered to the IBM electric typewriter and, finally, to the electronic word processor. In the final tally, however, these modernizations were only surface changes, cosmetic updating of the same nature as new cars or new refrigerators. The one thing no futurist could have foreseen in the 1960's was the coming of the desktop computer!

The invention of the desktop, personal computer drew the line of demarcation between what had been and what was to be. The power of those early machines (which, by comparison with today's, would seem like comparing the Model T Ford to a new BMW), was enormous! Office technology was off and running, never to be the same again.

Each new year brought new ideas and radical concepts. What seemed like a good idea only six months ago would become obsolete six months later. Long-distance telephone service went from telling an operator the name of the city and the party to whom you wanted to speak to picking up a phone, dialing thirteen digits, and within seconds speaking to an associate in Tokyo or London. Then the real adventures started. Telex lines gave way to data lines, and within months it became possible to send a copy of a complete document across the world, exactly as it appeared on the original, in less time than it took to read this paragraph! Fax machines, WATS lines, desk terminals, modems, plus a computer literate work force, equalled the greatest business change since the Industrial Revolution. And it happened in less then a decade! The answer to "Why now?," lies in Sir Edmund P. Hillary's answer when asked why he climbed Mount Everest: "Because it's there!" Today, for the first time in our history, we can communicate anywhere in the world, with any person we choose, with a minimal amount of preparation, and with virtually no third party necessary to complete the transaction. The day of "think and do" is upon us.

Other factors have also changed. We enjoy the dubious distinction of employing the oldest work force ever gathered on the face of the earth. By the year 2000, the average age of the work force will be thirty-nine. Three years older than the work forces' average age in 1991. This is partially as a result of a declining birth rate, partially due to better health care, and partially due to a decreased availability of qualified employees, America finds itself facing a graying work force.

This is not a negative factor however. The propensity toward an aging work force will have a sobering effect on the maturity and work ability of that force. Middle-aged workers want different benefits from their job than those which their younger counterparts seek. They want not only retirement and health benefits, but life benefits as well. They want more from life, from their jobs, and from their families. Their fathers were workaholics, company men who keeled over dead from heart attacks while working late instead of having dinner with their families. While the middle-aged worker may reject the values of the work ethic of the Fifties, remember that today's fifty-year-old executive was a flower child in the Sixties.

These workers are the "baby boomers" who were born following World War II. They've several characteristics in common, none of which, on the surface, seem to indicate that they'd be desirable employees. This generation has little or no loyalty to their employers but are extremely loyal to their team or their projects. They tend to regard themselves as apart from the company, but closely aligned with their fellow workers. Secondly, they have virtually no respect for hierarchy. They dislike being told what to do, almost as much as they dislike telling others what to do. And thirdly, they absolutely do not think of themselves as company men, but rather as independent thinkers. They would kill for the chance of owning their own company, and in the interim, they don't intend to kill themselves making someone else wealthy.

This may make older workers seem less desirable. However, their experience, their education, and their innate sense of proper conduct can more than make up for what may be perceived as a less than enthusiastic attitude. These very traits, conversely, are the traits that will make this worker an excellent candidate for telecommuting.

Age isn't the only factor that is changing the work force. Race, gender, and national origins are taking a hand in the newly defined labor pool. By the year 2000, workers between the ages of sixteen and twenty-two entering the job market for the first time will drop by almost two million, representing a total decline of almost 8 percent. Interestingly, well over 60 percent of the new workers will be females. Almost 30 percent of these new workers will not be caucasian; the majority will be Asian.

These facts point to still another factor working in favor of the older worker. They will require less supervision and, because of their level of maturity, are more likely to give their job their full attention and concentration. The concentration level of an older worker is especially important when the subject of telecommuting is considered. The very nature of telecommuting demands a higher ability to work without succumbing to the many interruptions which can plague the home-based worker. When we couple this mature worker with the technological advances that the Nineties offer, we find an idea whose time has come!

# Who's Using Telecommuting Now?

Telecommuting is being implemented by both the private and public sector. Because of the solitary nature of most jobs that lend themselves to this style of management, opportunity abounds for implementation within certain key industries. Insurance corporations, companies concerned with the design, installation and application of computer programming as well as companies which rely heavily on large amounts of data input, such as financial institutions, credit management concerns, publish-

subscription requests, sales orders, payment data entry, and shipping and warehousing businesses, are just a few of the multitude of private concerns which find telecommuters to be yet another arrow in their arsenal of personnel development.

Insurance companies have lead the nation in the use of telecommuters. Because so much of what an insurance company deals with is raw data, the need for imputing this data is critical. The Travelers Company, located in Hartford, Connecticut, is the primary example of what a dedicated program of telecommuters can do. In a later chapter, this company's commitment to telecommuting will be fully studied.

Surprising, however, is the speed in which the public sector has embraced telecommuting. Leading the nation in both research and planning is California. Both the state and a large number of municipalities have projects underway to study the feasibility of telecommuting as an alternative work style. It is logical that if any single state would feel an urgency to try this new management tool, it would be the state with the worst traffic congestion problem in the nation.

Other states are also in the process of studying and evaluating the possibility of telecommuting for their employees. An interesting fact is that not a single study thus far concluded has found telecommuting to be anything less than desirable. In most studies, the results far exceeded the stated goals. There are no losers in telecommuting. The worker, the employer, and even society in general wins.

# How Telecommuting Increases Productivity

The company that employs a telecommuting program can expect gains in several major areas.

The greatest area in which your company will benefit is in the field of productivity. The first concern voiced by most traditional managers when faced with the possibility of managing workers who telecommute is, "How will I know my employees are working?" This question is an exercise is futility. The answer is simple: how does a manager know now if his workers are producing? Is the fact that an employee can be found sitting at his or her desk *prima facie* evidence of diligence or productivity? Of course not! The way we assess any employee and his ability to produce is not by his physical presence, but rather by his production.

Modern managers manage by objectives, not by activity. It would be ludicrous to assess any worker's productivity by merely observing how many hours that worker spends bent over his keyboard or sitting at a drafting table. Sales managers do not count production by the number of sales calls made, but rather by the number of orders written. Likewise, other managers consider the volume of work completed, and completed properly, to be the yardstick against which productivity is measured.

In the traditional office setting, quotas are established for most workers. If that worker is a data entry person, a certain amount of forms are expected to be entered into his or her terminal each hour, or each day. Some sort of criteria is established by which the manager is able to determine if a particular employee is average, above average, or below average. If this were not done, then once any person had secured a position with a company, that job would be his or hers for life. By constant evaluation, the weaker workers are weeded out, the better workers are recognized, rewarded, and promoted. So it is with telecommuters.

The mere fact that an employee is not directly under the watchful eye of a supervisor does not make that worker any less sensitive to the fact that production schedules must be met and quotas must be filled. Conversely, inasmuch as there is no visible "authority" figure watching over a worker's shoulder, the lack of direct supervision may well make the worker much more productive. The proof of production, in the absence of a manager hovering over a worker, falls squarely on that worker.

While considering productivity, it would be well to consider the distractions within the office environment which tend to make a worker less productive. The degree of socialization which occurs during the normal work day is incredible! When workers first arrive at the office, they gather around the coffee machine, exchange pleasantries, swap war stories about that morning's freeway traffic, and share the events of the previous evening with each other. When they finally do settle down at their work stations, they spend another ten minutes or so "getting in gear" before they actually begin the business day. Somewhere around mid-morning, they may assemble again at the coffee machine or the water fountain and again engage each other in what can only be described as mindless chatter. After the mid-morning break, they once more return to their desks and again will spend a few more minutes getting back into the work mode.

Lunch provides another opportunity to completely forget about the day's activities and begin another period of socialization. It lasts anywhere from thirty minutes to a full hour after which the lingering thoughts from that non-business interruption (an interruption which now gives the worker things to consider other than the business at hand) pervade the thoughts and actions of your "present" employee. The afternoon break repeats the actions of the previous two interruptions that occurred earlier in the day. From that point on, the main considerations of the employee are the need to finish the "quota," and the anxiety of confronting long delays in rush-hour traffic.

And this is supposed to be the ideal employee! Now consider this. By some stroke of luck, a person is hired who does a really conscientious job, who considers the work at hand to be the most important aspect of his or her day. How long will that employee last in the face of all the others, who by now realize that their production could be greater, but are comfortable with doing 80 percent or 70 percent or perhaps as low as 50 percent of what they are capable of doing? Faced with this attitude, most managers will likely lower their expectations, and by extension, lower the true potential of their employees.

No one, short of Ebenezer Scrooge, would seriously advocate taking away the rights or privileges that the modern office workers have come to expect as part of their employment environment. Nor does anyone wish to make the workplace a hostile battlefield, pitting the manager against the worker, but some semblance of reason must take place. And telecommuting could be that bit of reasoning that will allow managers to once again take control without the use of a whip and bullhorn.

The workers who work at home know what is expected of them. They will meet or exceed that expectation for several reasons primarily because they cannot look about and see others doing less work than they are doing. The level of productivity rises when workers are isolated from one another. This can be carried too far, of course, and the dangers which arise out of this aspect of telecommuting will be discussed in another chapter.

# Eliminating Unnecessary Expenses

If a worker works at home, then a desk, a phone, a space, is not required for that worker in the main office. While this may seem terribly simple on the surface, consider the savings involved in this fact. Fewer workers in the office translates to less office space to rent, to furnish, and to provide environmental conditions for, such as heat and air conditioning. It means fewer restroom facilities, less water consumption, less electrical usage, less maintenance and less clean-up time. Less expense equals more profit! And profit is the bottom line.

A secondary factor to consider is that almost all expenses carry with them some form of taxation. If a corporation owns its building, then it must pay *ad valorem* taxes on that property. Since it takes almost twice as much work space for a hundred employees as it does fifty, the actual size of the office can be scaled down to allow for the decrease in square footage needed, a savings of considerable tax dollars each January.

Property taxes on one hundred desks are twice the amount due on fifty desks. Extend this concept to chairs, to chair mats, to break-room facilities, and the list is literally endless.

Shifting workers to telecommuting is not the same as laying off workers. A lay off of 50 percent of your work force would be the result (or the beginning) of a serious downturn in business. Indeed, it would probably foretell the beginning of the end for your business. There is a trick to downscaling your at-office workers, while increasing your telecommuting team. This plan must be carefully worked in order to allow the downsizing of office space and furniture. Done improperly, the costs of heating, cooling, and maintaining the facility would remain virtually unchanged. But by phasing in a home workers plan, within an eighteen month period, the savings and growth possibilities will begin to manifest themselves on the bottom line of the company's profit and loss statement.

# Hiring the Handicapped

There is a hidden benefit in any telecommuting program, and one that is seldom discussed. As our nation moves toward a recognition of the rights of the handicapped to equal employment, it is a given that within a few more years there will be some sort of congressional action requiring an affirmative action program toward this segment of our population. Even now, buildings are being designed to eliminate architectural barriers to wheelchairs and other artificial devices of mobility.

It is unfortunate that in our society the young, the attractive, and the physically healthy are given preference over the disabled. Common sense tells us that a handicapped individual is not necessarily a less viable employee. Yet, human nature being what it is often relegates these people to less than desirable jobs—if jobs can be found at all!

There can be no doubt, however, that a wheelchair bound individual, with sound mental faculties and a desire to earn a decent living, could fit well into a telecommuter situation. This is a solution to a problem which will not soon go away, and it can have a two-pronged effect. First, it could provide a good job to an individual who might otherwise become dependent upon society. In addition, it would stem the sure and certain tide of legislation—that awaits American business in the coming decade—concerning the hiring policies of large corporations which depend heavily on government contracts.

## Increasing the Pool

There is yet another labor pool from which a company with a telecommuter program can benefit. There are individuals, for one reason or another, who absolutely refuse to relocate to a different city, or state, or in some cases, a different country. These individuals may be experts, authorities if you will, on certain aspects which would directly effect the productivity of a particular corporation. If they could be hired or lured into the corporate world which your company seeks to dominate, it would be not only a feather in your cap, but could, in some cases, mean the difference in a company's survival or demise. With a telecommuting program already in place, there would be no problem in offering employment to the individual in question. Once more, a telecommuting program could be the decisive edge that will place your company ahead of your competition.

This works both ways. If an employee, a key person within an organization, is faced with an unexpected situation which would require that he or she relocate, your company might be forced to lose the services of that individual. However, if a telecommuting program already exists, this situation shifts from a crisis in management to one of simple logistics.

# Environmental Impact

Another factor for corporate consideration is the issue of environmental concerns. It is no longer reasonable nor responsible for any corporation to take the position that the environment is not its concern. This problem is one which faces all companies as they deal with a more informed populace.

Your company does not have to dump toxic waste into schoolyards or discard nuclear by-products into old folk's homes to be accused of being insensitive to the problems of pollution and resource wasting! Moreover, governmental agencies are now beginning to hold corporations responsible for the number of automobiles they attract to major areas of traffic congestion.

California is leading the nation in an attempt to blame corporate America for being the culprit behind traffic congestion and air pollution. Before any new construction can begin in Los Angeles County, it is now mandatory for the contractors to submit a plan to the county commission detailing how traffic will be reduced, or at least not increased, attendant to the construction of that building.

# Preparation for Natural Disasters

There is yet another factor to consider when deciding whether or not to implement a telecommuting program. Natural occurrences and natural disasters can strike without warning. Ice storms can keep the normal commuter at home—sometimes for days at a time. Floods, tornados, and, as evidenced in 1989 in San Francisco, earthquakes can reduce a thriving business to a mere handful of management personnel with little more to do than play solitaire until the roads are cleared and traffic can resume its normal pace.

After an earthquake is not the time to try to implement a telecommuting project! Contingency planning is just that—planning before the emergency is upon us.

# Employee Benefits from Telecommuting

Many of the same benefits enjoyed by management are also enjoyed by the employees who volunteer to engage in a telecommuting program. The word that must be stressed is "volunteer." Few workers forced into a telecommuting project will be successful. In fact, not all workers who request the opportunity to telecommute should be given the chance. In chapter 7, the telecommuter's profile is discussed. But for purposes of understanding what an employee will get out of the program, let's consider some of the advantages telecommuting offers the worker who will fit the profile.

# Increased Productivity

To fully understand why telecommuting can increase productivity, we must first look at the average workers' work day. Long before he or she arrives at the office preparations must be made which have little or nothing to do with the actual work that the employee will do that day. A woman must select her clothes, apply her make-up, fix her hair, and if she has children, fairly or not, she will probably be the prime mover of those children toward either school or the day-care center. All this must be completed, and then she still must contend with transportation to work. In the case of a male employee, little differs in his routine. He must arise, shave, dress, help with the children, perhaps actually providing the transportation for those children, and then manage to commute to the office as well. All this must be done so that the employee is at his or her desk at the appointed hour—somewhere between eight and nine o'clock in the morning.

When your employees finally do sit at their desks, they are already tired. They have faced an ordeal better suited for a marine drill sergeant than for an executive, and now, they are expected to do an about-face, forget the hassles of the morning, and settle directly into a productive work mode.

Now imagine the same scenario, sans the mad rush to the office. How much more productive would they be if they simply skipped the tedious and non-productive drive to work. Statistically, the average commute to and from work is approximately forty minutes each way. In the case of Los Angeles, Houston, New York, New Orleans, and Boston that drive averages fifty-six minutes. This amounts to a minimum of 375 hours per year spent traveling between home and office. Considering the average work week is forty hours, each commuter spends almost an extra ten weeks per year just going back and forth between home and work. What if the commute was eliminated and the worker spent even half that time engaged in productive activities? The result would be an increase of a minimum of 10 percent more output, at no additional cost to the employer. Raising productivity by 10 percent is the stuff of which managers dream, and with telecommuting, that dream becomes a reality!

And remember, this is a minimum increase. Realistically, an employer can expect an even greater increase in productivity, in many cases as high as 20 to 30 percent.

# The Cost of Going to Work

Getting there may be half the fun on a vacation, but it certainly isn't fun when it comes to getting to work. An employee who drives fifteen miles each way between the office and home drives 7,500 miles each year. Because of the nature of commuter driving, gas mileage is extremely low. City drivers can expect an average of thirteen miles per gallon of gas. The yearly commute to work will cost the commuter in the neighborhood of 600 gallons of gas per year, per car. Even with car pooling, this is an awful lot of gas and an extremely expensive proposition. Our commuter can fully expect to spend about $800 per year in fuel expenses alone. This of course does not take into account either the wear on his or her automobile (items such as tires, oil) or the general depreciation of his or her vehicle.

# Tangible Savings Relating to Employment

Consider the cost of clothing. According to the National Association of Dry Cleaners, the average men's suit (of which the average male middle-level executive owns six) will require dry cleaning at least sixteen times per year, at an average cost of $5.75 per suit. His five favorite ties will see the cleaner at least once each month, another $1.50 per tie, per month. If he sends his shirts out to be laundered, chalk up another $1.00 per day. Just keeping his clothes cleaned and pressed will represent an expense of well over $500 per year. And this doesn't include the cost of replacement garments, new shirts, new suits, new ties, and new shoes.

Wardrobe maintenance and upgrading for a middle level executive can easily cost $1000 per year! A female executive's wardrobe, partially due to the frequency of fashion changes and the nature of the fabrics used in their design, can run an additional 50 percent more.

Add to these costs the fees involved in toll roads, parking lots, and parking permits, and the cost of just going to work can amount to 10 to 20 percent of an employee's salary! Eliminate the daily commute and your company's compensation package suddenly increases radically, without the expenses incurred by an increase in pay. Saving $2000 per year is better than a raise of the same amount. There are no taxes to be paid on savings!

It would be impossible to calculate in dollars the savings in stress and pressures, but there certainly must be a correlation between the two. Telecommuting will result in a more relaxed worker, one who can give more and better time to his job. The result of this is likely to be a more tranquil, happier employee, and a happy employee is one who is both more likely to retain his or her job, and to value his or her employment. The psychological edge this can give a worker cannot be measured in dollars and cents, but it will certainly be measured in increased production!

# Other Factors Impact the Corporate Employee

There are other factors which must be considered when a telecommuting program is implemented. Family relations—that is, the nature of the relationship between both the spouse of the employee and his or her children—can increase or decrease the amount of productivity a worker generates. Farmers enjoy the lowest divorce rate of all occupations. Why? It could well be that despite the economic woes which often beset a farming business, it is an occupation which usually allows the husband and the wife, as well as the children, to remain in close proximity to each other. The one factor which remains constant in a farmer's life is that he will be home for lunch! While this may seem superficial, consider the stability which this type of arrangement fosters. This is not to suggest that the answer to the soaring divorce rate in America is due in total to the fact that the marriage partners are apart for long periods of time. Rather it does imply that the two primary individuals involved in the relationship—that is, the husband and the wife—see each other on a regular basis, and because of this, stronger lines of personal communications may be formed.

Sociologists and other professionals which deal with the breakdown of the family unit generally concede a definite relationship between the amount of time spouses are apart to the growing tendency toward broken homes. In the earlier half of this century, divorce was a relatively rare event. In those days, people either worked at home, such as farmers or auto mechanics, or were often engaged in some form of a cottage industry. At most, their jobs were often within ten minutes of where they lived. In today's high-tech society, workers find they must daily fight for a traffic lane, fight for a parking spot, and fight to grab a quick sandwich at the local lunch counter, and the divorce rate has reached 50 percent! Certainly, a parallel can be drawn.

No one is advocating telecommuting as a way to save marriages; but clearly, a worker going through domestic problems cannot possibly be expected to be as productive as a happily married individual would be. Telecommuting benefits the community as well. If a worker must commute to work, he or she finds less time to spend with his or her children. This can manifest itself in less time spent in his or her community.

Lack of community involvement will many times transform itself into community apathy; it will take the form of a lack of interest in the school system, the local government, and other issues which tend to bond the individual to his or her community. When this results, a lack of commitment will become a lack of "roots," which can, in turn, tend to make the worker feel less loyal toward his or her place of employment. After all, one unhappy place is the same as another. But substitute that lack of interest for a feeling of belonging and participation, and the worker who might have at one time contemplated changing jobs and moving to another city will consider his or her community involvement in making any such decision. This may be the final element which determines whether an employee stays where he or she is or seeks employment elsewhere, resulting in your company having to replace, retrain, and rebuild the relationship once enjoyed with the previous employee.

Remember, the first four months of a new employee's training will negate the profitability of that employee for nine months! If an employee is productive and profitable, any edge your company can have in regard to retaining that worker is an edge worth exploring. Starting over is more than an inconvenience, it's downright costly!

# Benefits which Both Labor and Management Share

There are many benefits which are shared by both the corporation and the employees. These benefits, while not necessarily benefits which each party enjoys for the same reasons, nevertheless result in an overall improvement of society in general.

# Reduced Pollution

Pollution requires government action, which in turn usually results in government regulation. Any effort to reduce pollution, and certainly automobiles are the major source of pollution in most metropolitan areas, will result in a lessening of government restrictions as well as providing a cleaner and safer environment. The very appearance of concern about pollution can result in excellent public relations toward the company which initiates such actions. Further, it fosters general feelings of well-being and pride among employees of that corporation.

Studies indicate that in most geographic locales, car pooling, telecommuting, and flexible work hours all contribute to a lessening of fluorocarbons in the air. (San Francisco is the notable exception. The preponderance of downtown attractions is a great draw to those living in the outlying Bay area.) Therefore, upon installing a telecommuting program, it is advantageous for your corporation to make sure that your community becomes aware that your company is actively seeking a way to help fight air pollution.

# Mass Transit

The total cost for public transportation is not borne entirely by those using it. Quite the contrary, most metropolitan areas require the city or the transit authority to subsidize the cost of operating the systems. These entities have no way of producing that excess revenue other than through taxes, and these taxes usually fall on the back of the corporate community. While buses, rapid area transit systems, and even subways are convenient and often inexpensive ways to shuttle the worker between his or her home and the workplace, they still are extremely expensive to maintain.

Beyond the cost of the actual vehicle, there is, of course, the cost of fuel, maintenance, and rail or roadway upkeep. In the cases of both underground systems and elevated rails, there are additional costs of security and police protection to safeguard the commuters and protect the property against vandals. Add to this employee salaries, both for the actual operators as well as the support personnel, and the cost of a subway token becomes the deal of the century. The additional costs for these systems are borne by the tax-paying entities of the city which they serve. These additional taxes are passed on to the consumer in the form of increased costs for the goods and services which the corporation provides. Increased costs lead to increased prices which often can result in decreased sales, hence, decreased profits.

## Security as a Factor in the Metropolitan Environment

There is an inherent security risk in riding a subway to work. Admittedly, the risk diminishes during rush hours, and also with the availability of certain types of mass transit, such as trolley or bus service. But that risk does exist, and crime rates are not decreasing! Each time an employee of any corporation sets foot on public conveyance, that person runs the risk of assault, robbery, or worse. This is a classic example of telecommuting serving the same cause but with two different motivations. Telecommuters are safer because generally they are not exposed to random urban violence. This benefits the commuter. And the company is safer because its employees, which in a practical sense are assets, are not put at as much risk.

The likelihood of getting mugged between one's bedroom and one's study are much less than that of riding a bus to work and then walking three blocks to an office building. Even parking in a secured area is no guarantee of safety. Well after the worker is in his or her car and clear of the company parking lot, there is still considerable risk to him or her between the job site and his or her home.

# Reduced Dependence of Foreign Petroleum

Events in the recent years have shown time and time again that with very little provocation, Americans, as well as their European counterparts, can suddenly find themselves hostage to rising oil prices. For the telecommuter, the price of gasoline becomes less of a concern. The result of this is, of course, a reduction in consumption of petroleum products. This is a two-fold benefit. Less petrol usage results in less pollution, and conversely, a larger supply of fuel, in turn, generally results in lower prices for that which we do consume.

All petrochemical product usage declines with the widespread use of telecommuting. Gasoline, oil, grease, solvents, lubricants, and even tires and other rubber based items which use petrochemicals as a basis for manufacture are conserved. This reduces the demand for these products, hence limiting the possibility of shortages of these nonrenewable energy sources.

# Social and Personal Situational Benefits

There are literally dozens of reasons why telecommuting can make a worker more productive. Latch-key kids become less susceptible to dangers which they now face when they arrive home to an empty house. Residential burglaries decrease when a house is occupied during the day, when well over half of all homes are robbed.

In an aging society, more and more adult children are becoming responsible for and the primary care providers of their elderly parents. Commuting to the city each day, leaving the elderly to fend for themselves, often results in situations which lead to anxiety on both the part of the adult child and the aged parent. Telecommuting can alleviate this concern. This concern for the family unit can also be perceived by the community as a humanizing factor on the part of the corporation which, in addition to all the other benefits which accompany telecommuting, should be publicized and promoted to allow the corporation to capitalize on the goodwill such a program will create within the community.

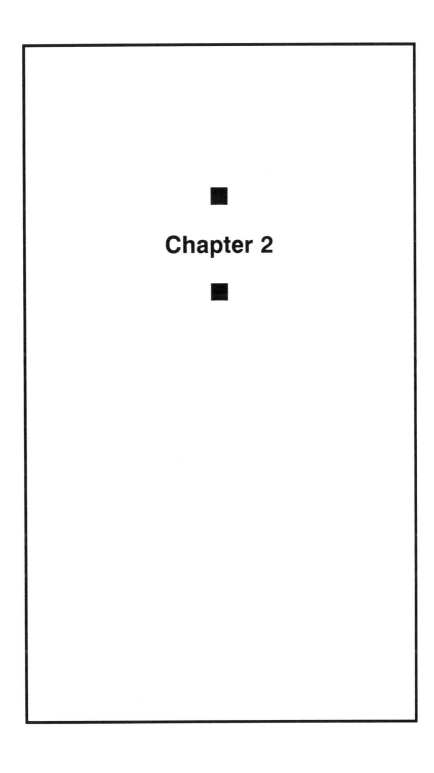

# Chapter 2

# Finding the Right Personnel and Project to Implement a Telecommuting Program

**P**rofiles of a Telecommuter and the Problems Attendant to the Program

Telecommuters are made not born. There are certain character traits, however, that lend themselves to making a successful telecommuter. Perhaps the overall catch-word would be maturity. A worker who must have constant supervision is not likely to suddenly develop the self-discipline required to be a home worker.

## Self-Starters

The ability to begin work without the presence of a supervisor is not one that all people possess. Certain fields of employment, however, lend themselves to the development of this type of an employee. Researchers have found that sales people, data entry personnel, as well as most creative endeavors—for example, computer program design, statistical analysis, various aspects of advertising, art mock-up, and graphic presentations, tend to do well in the realm of telecommuting. The very act of telecommuting requires a certain blend of confidence, intelligence, and professionalism most often found in these fields.

## Job Experience

Certainly, job experience is a major factor in determining who should be a telecommuter and who should not. The Travelers, a pioneer in telecommuting, make it a company policy not to hire a telecommuter at the entry level. The reason for this is fairly obvious. One cannot be expected to do a good job at home if one doesn't know how to do the job at the office. For this reason, most telecommuters have been with their company for a minimum of six months, in many cases much longer than that, before telecommuting can be considered an optional mode of employment.

Obviously, technical training is more easily conducted from the central office than it would be from a remote location. The tools for training, such as printers, computers, and diagnostic analytical equipment, tend to be concentrated in the central office. Moreover, the managerial staff, the actual training instructors as well as the supervisory personnel, all will find teaching from the central location more cost and time efficient. Once the training period is complete and the technical information has been imparted to the potential telecommuter, then that employee could be considered a candidate for home working.

Note: *Not all good office personnel make good telecommuters.* Telecommuting, while not a viable option for or equally applicable to all employees, should be made available as a reward to any employee who has shown the proper mix of ability, desire, and capability to perform this type of service.

## Communication Skills

Perhaps one of the greatest assets a telecommuter can possess is the ability to communicate effectively. In the rapidly developing age of information, only those who can communicate effectively will survive. Inter-office memos, voice mail, E-mail, and fax machines are all useful tools for long distance communications. But anyone who has ever read a three page fax knows that brevity is the soul of efficiency. It is, therefore, of key importance that persons engaged in any form of telecommuting hone their communication skills.

If an employee cannot get his or her point across to a manager while still in the office, there is little possibility that remoteness and distance will enhance his or her abilities.

Many companies employ daily or at least weekly meetings for the purpose of establishing the goals for that period of time. These meetings are often called budget or project meetings, sometimes they're merely called planning sessions. And they are necessary! They are necessary for two reasons. First, they help outline what is expected of the individual employee for that day or week. In addition, they outline what the company, as an entity, expects to achieve during that same period.

In law firms, these "progress" meetings serve as a time for all the partners to inform each other on the status of individual cases and to seek advice on any situation which may be potentially troublesome. In organizations where sales are the primary function of management, these "sales" meetings are held to establish quotas, to discuss future marketing plans, and to explore new product feasibility. The point is this. These meetings have worth and purpose, and now, as a telecommuter, your employees are not going to be attending them with the regularity they once did.

To make up for the lack of physical attendance, it is important, especially in the case of lower and middle level employees, that the lines of communications are kept open and clear. The art of memo writing will become just that, an art. Editing out extraneous information, useless statistics, and meaningless verbiage will become of prime importance when communicating with the worker who works off-site. Memos will become the mainstay of the new order of doing business. In a memo to your off-site worker, you must be precise, accurate, and concise.

## *Organization as a Way of Life*

The one overriding factor all telecommuters have in common is their ability to make the right decisions at the right time. This is a crucial trait, and without it, all the best intentions in the world won't be able to make up for the boondoggle that will eventually develop. Staying at home, doing a job, and turning in a steady stream of work is the ultimate goal of the telecommuter. But unlike their office-bound co-workers, they must go it alone. This means that in most cases there is no secretary to straighten the desk, to sort the mail, and to screen the calls. There is no junior assistant to handle the detail work which we all find so annoying. (Isn't that why God made junior assistants?) The plain and terrifying truth of the matter is that to be successful at telecommuting, the employee must be successful at organization.

Organization is not a dirty word, but it can be dirty work. Working at home is no reason to allow one's workspace to become cluttered or disorganized. Because an employee is at home, certain niceties which are often found on the desk at the office are unnecessary. We can dispense with the pictures of our spouse and children. (We live there, remember? We see them all day long!) Also extraneous is the "Thanks for not smoking" sign, as well as a nameplate, a business card holder, and the other trappings used to impress fellow workers and office visitors. This means the possibility for an orderly workspace is greatly enhanced, and so is the probability of a more productive day.

## *Organizing the Home Office*

The first consideration in working at home is picking the proper location for work. This is, in and of itself, a tricky proposition. To paraphrase a real estate maxim, three things are necessary for success: location, location, and location. The telecommuter should find a place where work can be conducted and conducted without interruption. A spare bedroom is ideal. Perhaps a room in the basement, or the attic, or even a converted outer building, such as a storage shed, a utility building, or a portion of a garage. There are, however, a multitude of considerations which need to be thought through. Problems such as heating and cooling, lighting, ventilation, and proximity to adequate electrical and phone lines must all be taken into consideration before a site is chosen.

Certain areas should be ruled out at the outset. The kitchen is perhaps the worst possible place to set up an office. An incredible amount of the day-to-day running of a home originates in the kitchen, and one of the primary objectives of the work station is that work not be packed up each evening and unpacked each morning. This would be tantamount to packing up your corporate office each night and unpacking it each morning when you return. It is not only a waste of time and effort, but it contributes nothing to production. Anything that does not aid in the production of the work flow inhibits it.

Likewise, it isn't prudent to establish a work area in a high traffic zone. Encourage your workers to stay away from high distraction areas. While soft FM music in the background may not be unnerving, a never ending series of soap operas and automobile commercials blaring from a television will indeed inhibit the continual production of work. Many managers also advise their home workers that the same room in which the worker sleeps makes a poor work area. The reason for this is obvious to anyone who has ever been forced to stay in a single place for a substancial length of time. Cabin fever sets in quickly; the sameness of the environment, coupled with the lack of social interaction soon results in a feeling of captivity, not unlike that of being sentenced to solitary confinement.

Encourage your workers to maintain a well lighted, well ventilated, comfortable work area—an area where, when the day's work is finished, the worker can walk away and leave his desk as it is. This makes the next day's task of starting to be one which is surmountable.

## Establishing a Schedule

An important aspect of telecommuting is making and keeping consistent and productive work habits. Many of the routine habits developed over years of reporting to work at an office at 9:00 a.m. are no longer applicable once an employee starts to telecommute. It is no longer necessary to rise at six in the morning, make a mad dash through a shower, gulp down a cup of coffee and a few slices of toast, and begin the harried commute to the office. Nor does it mean the worker will stay in bed until 8:45 and then pad into his or her office wearing his or her pajamas and then sign on to his or her computer terminal at 8:55. A new set of habits should be constructed around this new work style.

One advantage often cited by telecommuters is that they have more time to read the journals and technical publications applicable to their employment field with greater regularity. A stock broker, for example, will find he or she now has an extra hour to ingest investment publications and to study more closely the market reports than previously. Likewise, a salesperson will find more time to analyze trends in his or her industry, to read the competition's literature, and to seek chinks in their competitor's armor!

The point is this. While telecommuting eliminates a great deal of wasted time, that time is still wasted if the employee doesn't use it to enhance his expertise and job productivity.

## Becoming Comfortable in the New Environment

Of the better than two hundred telecommuters interviewed for this book, not one reported dressing formally for work on the days they telecommuted. Quite the contrary, most said they dressed as they would on any day they weren't planning on going into the office. This meant blue jeans, flannel shirts, and tennis shoes. Ties were left in the closet, along with panty hose, high heels, and business suits! One of the nicest aspects of telecommuting is that the employee can be more concerned with how his production looks than how well his tie coordinates with his shirt!

It should be emphasized that this can be carried to the other extreme. Just as most of us would not show up at the office wearing a tuxedo or formal gown, neither should the home worker sit around in his boxer shorts or night shirt. Encourage your telecommuter to maintain a semblance of decorum, at least enough to remind himself that the purpose of working at home is to produce work!

As important as starting the day right is ending it right. It is very important that your employee have a designated stopping time. The temptation to continue working well past the normal quitting time will be great. As strange as this may seem, the telecommuting employees will develop the feeling that since the work is still there, and so are they, they might as well continue working. While it is impossible to force telecommuters to stop working and relax, it is important that they understand that you expect just that. The threat of burnout is as real, if not more so, to telecommuters as it is to any other workers.

It's a good idea to suggest to your employees that they develop a ritual concerning the end of the work day. Some things they can do to signal that the day is over is to leave their work center, to change clothes (or at least shoes), and perhaps even to leave the house for a short time. A walk around the block, a short trip to the market, or even just watching the evening news can signal that the work day is finished. After this routine is established, it will become easier for the telecommuter to stop working and enjoy his or her leisure time.

## Establishing a Regimen

Just as a daily routine is required in the formal office, one is required in the home office as well. As stressed earlier, communications becomes the focal point of most telecommuters' lives. There is a great deal of technological equipment available to assist your employees in establishing their office at home, but perhaps none is more important than an answering machine. In the corporate office, if an employee leaves his or her work station, someone will cover the phone. When your employee starts to work at home and steps away from his or her desk, it is likely that no one will be available to answer the phone.

A caller has no way of knowing how long the phone will remain unanswered—for a few minutes or the whole day. This can result in a great many problems, especially since the caller may not be aware the person he's calling is working at home. As far as the caller is concerned, there is no way to leave word that he called. The frustration behind this can often result in loss of business, and in some cases, it can even result in driving the caller to the arms of a competitor. This problem is easily remedied by the installation of an answering machine. One indicator of how radically technology has changed the habits of the American businessman is the fact that just a few years ago people considered it demeaning and rude to have to leave a message on a tape recorder. Today, if no one answers after several rings, the caller is offended by that party's ambivalence—that is, that there is no machine to take a message.

The degree of technological sophistication that will be required to support your employee's efforts from home will depend to a large extent on the nature of that person's job. To be certain, if the home worker is a data entry clerk, then a computer, along with a modem to facilitate the downloading of imputted information is mandatory. However, a fax machine may not be mandated in such a scenario. Conversely, if the primary function of the telecommuter is to analyze contractual phraseology or work on graphics for advertising campaigns, it would be next to impossible to function without the use of a fax transmitter. Basically, what your company provides for the telecommuter will depend to a great degree on that worker's job.

## *Adapting Others to the Telecommuter's Environment*

Adjustments to the telecommuter's new environment will not only be limited to the employee and his or her manager. There is an education process which will need take place within the home both with his or her family and his or her friends. The novelty of working at home will soon give way to a regular routine similar to that which the worker formerly experienced at the central work place. In a matter of days or perhaps a few weeks, the worker will become accustomed to working at home. The hardest aspect of this new situation will come when those who live with or near the telecommuter realize that a whole new set of rules and regulations come with the presence of the telecommuter—rules that never before faced the family.

The telecommuter's spouse may view having his or her mate home as either an adventure in intimacy or a detriment to his or her daily routine. Before this new style of working began, a telecommuter's spouse—generally, his wife—in all probability had already established her own routine, her own way of getting through the day. Perhaps she would do all her housework as soon as her husband and children left for work and school and then spend the remainder of the day watching soaps. (Someone must be watching them!) Or perhaps she would spend the morning on the phone with her friends, and devote the afternoon hours to her homemaking activities. Regardless of how she spent her days before the change to telecommuting took place, she now must consider the fact that her husband is now home at least three days a week, and there will be a period of adjustment that must take place.

This is particularly true when the telecommuter is a man. In most contemporary marriages, both partners have some sort of employment. At the risk of seeming chauvinistic, the primary income earner, according to the latest statistics available from the United States Department of Labor, is usually the man. In homes where the wife works, the husband's shift from office worker to telecommuter will likely not cause a great deal of domestic problems. Inasmuch as the wife is at work during the day anyway, her husband's presence in the home will not prove disruptive. This is not to say there won't be distractions—the tendency will be to consider the home worker as a person with extra time on his hands.

Care must be taken to avoid falling into the scenario which allows relatives and neighbors to assume that since the home worker is home anyway, he or she won't mind watching their kids for an hour, or becoming the designated recipient of all UPS deliveries for the neighborhood, or letting the television repair man into the house next door because the neighbor has a "real" job—one which requires them to be absent for the entire day. This is a real and present threat to the success of the telecommuter, one which his supervisor must caution the potential telecommuter to avoid.

However, it is a fact that most of these types of problems will occur in the first few weeks of the telecommuter's liberation from the office. It takes very little time for the newness of his situation to wear off and for the family and friends which surround him to realize that he is gainfully employed. Just as these people would not come to his office downtown and sit across from his desk for the sole purpose of engaging him in idle chit-chat, they can be educated to respect his need for privacy. The important thing to remember is that there is a period of adjustment which needs to be taken into consideration when preparing production guidelines and performance expectations for the new telecommuter.

### Managing the Manager

And what of the manager who previously managed twenty-five workers? He or she now has an office staff of five at-office employees and a phantom staff of twenty. Obviously, the five still there will be in need of supervision, but so will the twenty he or she can no longer see. He or she will still maintain an open line of communication between himself or herself and his or her workers; but now, instead of worrying about the small, petty politics of office infrastructure, his or her main concern is productivity.

He or she will maintain a close tie with all the workers, perhaps even closer than before, and do it with a greater degree of efficiency than had been previously thought possible.

A contented, fulfilled employee is a productive employee. An amazingly high percentage of workers who have opted for telecommuting say that they have never felt more positive about their jobs. A recent study conducted by the Department of Labor for the State of California reported that out of 200 workers who were temporarily assigned telecommuting positions, 177 requested the change to be permanent. That's a conversion rate of 89 percent! Overall, production from these employees was up 23 percent, and in some individual cases, the increases were as high as 44 percent.

Morale was cited most often as the primary reason for increased productivity. For the first time in their careers, many of the telecommuters felt that they were trusted by management to do a good job. That trust inspired them to strive to new heights of production.

A survey conducted by the Harvard School of Business in 1989 indicated the primary reason cited for a change of employment, a reason listed in well over 45 percent of all responses, was a lack of job satisfaction. Telecommuting can and does give workers that sense of satisfaction. It gives him or her the opportunity to prove his or her worth as well as an incentive to continue to improve his or her quality of performance.

## *Profile of the Telecommuting Manager*

The purpose of a manager is not to manage, but rather to attain pre-stated and predetermined results. The psychological problems facing a traditional office manager when he or she is suddenly confronted with a staff which no longer works in the office can seem overwhelming. Initially it is to feel that he or she is no longer needed. Nothing could be further from the truth. Long distance managing is perhaps the most difficult form of management because it strips the manager of any and all extraneous activities; the manager must focus squarely on the purpose for which he or she was hired. Management's production must now be measured, not by activity, but by its results. Getting results was the reason that individual was given managerial responsibility to begin with. He or she was put in charge of a staff of workers, and given his or her orders. *Produce!*

Many managers allow themselves to become mired in the day-to-day skirmishes of office politics. They find they must coddle one worker while chiding another. They walk a fine line of being perceived as either Simon Legree or Simple Simon. With their workers away from their immediate sphere of influence, many managers fear loss of control. In reality, the opposite is most often the case. They do not lose control of their employees. Rather, they suddenly find themselves able to do that for which they were hired—and with a higher level of success than they previously dreamed possible. They suddenly find themselves managing for the first time. One of the many side benefits of telecommuting is that absenteeism drops to near zero. The worker who occasionally doesn't come into the office because he wants to stay home is already home. And since he is already home, he might as well work. Situations that would have prevented a worker from being at the office, such as allergies, colds, inclement weather, and oversleeping, which would have resulted in his being late anyway, suddenly disappear as a viable reason for not working.

These factors may well be the reason telecommuters have a tendency to higher production figures. With many occupations, such as data entry or computer programing, workers find themselves starting at six or seven in the morning. They accomplish more in the first five hours of the day than they previously did in a regular eight hour workday.

The telecommuting manager must ask himself one basic question. Do I really care if my employee works for a full eight hours and produces the assigned task given him or do I want full production plus 10 to 15 percent more? The bottom line is this. Managers who manage by activity are really nothing more than kindergarten teachers who stand over the desk of five-year olds and make sure they color their pictures. Managers who manage by results are the ones who make a profit for their company and, by extension, place themselves in line for promotions and bonuses. Only the most inept managers would chose the former instead of the later.

## Communicating the Expectations of the Job to the Telecommuter

The communications skills of the telecommuting manager is the key to his or her success. Communication comes in many forms; but, for the manager of a telecommuting staff, it is imperative that his or her skills be sharply honed. For the man or woman who manages his or her staff via fax machines and phone lines, there can be little room for unclear directives or fuzzy communiques. There are certain basic guidelines to follow when managing a team of telecommuters.

(1) All communication between the central office and the telecommuter must be precise and accurate. Many ideas are communicated between boss and employee not only by the spoken word, but by the other less obvious forms of communication. Body language, facial expressions, and even mannerisms as subtle as straighting papers on a desk or closing a date book can tell the employee a great deal about what his manager is saying. In telecommuting, the subtleties don't exist. What you read or what you hear is what you get. It is imperative, therefore, that all instructions are written as clearly as possible. In the past, when a manager has given his or her sub-

ordinates unclear directives, he or she was able to cover his or her own ineptness by claiming employee error. In the telecommuting world, there can be no such excuse. Every directive is in writing!

(2) A new state of trust must exist between management and labor. This trust must be predicated on the fact that both parties share the same objective, that is, optimum productivity coupled with professional competency. If the telecommuting manager cannot operate on the premise that his or her employees are sincere and responsible individuals, he or she needs to rethink his or her hiring policies. They are managers, not policemen. To continue to think that the only way to squeeze an assignment out of a worker is to stand over him or her is equivalent to believing that the only way to power a ship is with sails. This concept of telecommuting is new and exciting. It calls for the best in both the employer and the employee!

(3) Contact between the worker and his supervisor is crucial. The best worker in the world can go off track without some form of supervision. Contact your employee on a regular basis. Let him know that you are there not only to check and supervise the quality of his or her work, but also to clarify and assist in the definition and execution of his or her projects. Never, never, go a week without checking the progress (or lack thereof) of each telecommuting staff member! As a manager, you must show trust and confidence in your worker; but at the same time, you are ultimately responsible for seeing that all projects are completed on time and within budget. This is not a contradiction in concepts. By the very nature of allowing telecommuting to exist within

the framework of your department, you have indicated a willingness to trust your employee's judgement. But that doesn't mean you must check your brains at the door when you come to work. Remain in close and constant contact, not as a watchdog, but as a mentor.

(4) Keep the employee as current as possible on what is going on at the office. Isolation can lead to serious problems in any telecommuting project. Contact can be maintained in a number of ways. Confer with all the workers at a specific time, either at the beginning of the day or near the end of the afternoon. This will allow interaction without causing a great deal of disturbance to a telecommuter's workday. The phone call can be arranged for a particular day at a particular time, and all staff members can be in attendance, very much like a regular staff meeting held in a more traditional office.

Periodically, it is an excellent idea to bring the entire staff—both telecommuting and office staff—physically together to discuss the problems and objectives of your department as they change. All staff members involved in the telecommuting department should attend such meetings if possible. Obviously, if your telecommuting staff is spread all across the United States, then a full scale, sit-down meeting may only be possible once or twice a year. If, however, all are located within, say, fifty or seventy miles of the central office, then sit-down meetings should be held on a more regular basis.

As we will see when we examine specific projects conducted by various companies across America, the exact dynamics of any telecommuting conferences will vary widely; however, they will all have one thing in common. Periodically, they all do come together! It is these regular meetings that bond a cohesive and competent staff into a productive and energetic telecommuting department.

(5) Never treat your telecommuting employees like second class employees! This may seem obvious; but, there is a proclivity toward discrimination based on the fact that those employees who are not regularly seen in the office tend to be viewed as "extra" help, as opposed to an integral part of the corporate team. Certain measures should be taken to assure the telecommuters that in their absence they are not forgotten. In a recent study conducted by the Colorado Department of Employment, it was concluded that companies employing telecommuters tended to overlook these employees when promoting and giving pay raises. This discriminates against the very workers who are the most productive and the most likely to enable your company to increase its bottom line profits.

(6) The benefit package of the telecommuter should never in any way be different than the benefits offered an officed employee—with the possible exception of the reserved parking spot. In regard to vacation, sick leave, insurance packages, and other perks, the telecommuting employee should not take a back seat to the traditional commuter. It is essential to the well being of your telecommuting program that all those involved feel that they too are a part of the family of workers within your corporation. This is not just an act of fairness, it is good business. Any good employee is an asset to his firm; no smart manager mistreats his assets.

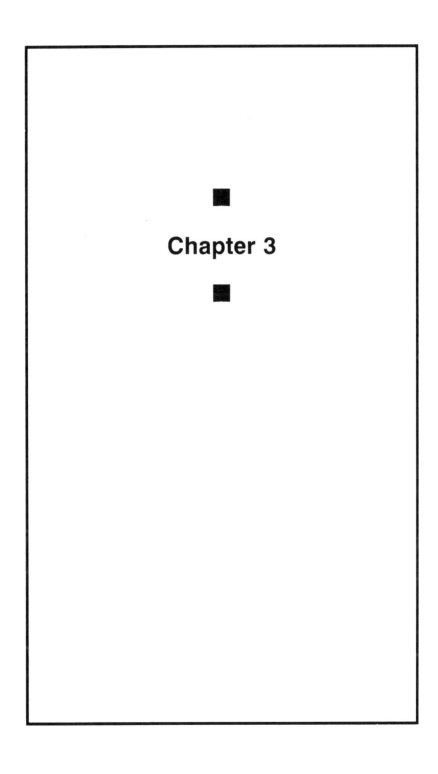

# Chapter 3

# How to Begin a
# Telecommuting Program

## Implementation of a
## Telecommuting Program

The question of costs must be considered when any company implements a telecommuting program. While the savings to both the company and the employee in regard to time and money are enormous, like any other new project, there will be start-up costs and downtime to consider. Try to see the implementation of a telecommuting system as a remodeling job at your current office. While the workmen are hammering, painting, hanging new doors, running wires, cables, and pipes throughout the office complex, there will be a certain amount of detractions and productivity loss. But the loss will not be permanent, and hopefully, because of the remodeling, that temporarily loss of productivity will be made up and additional future growth will be possible.

This is the same proposition faced by any company that proceeds with a telecommuting program. There will be additional costs and downtime and a temporary loss of production. These things are unavoidable, but they can be minimized with careful planning and some common sense precautions.

## Planning the Move

With the profile of the telecommuter firmly in mind, consider which of your personnel are the most likely candidates for the new program. Remember there are two primary criteria. First, the job, second, the worker. The best secretary in the world, the one with the greatest personality and the most finely honed people skills, cannot effectively do his or her job from his or her living room. Equally, the most efficient receptionist cannot greet incoming clients from her dining room table. The first consideration must be, "Can this job be done from any location other than where it is now being done?" If the answer is no, than this position is not appropriate for telecommuting.

However, if the answer to the test question is yes, then the next question is that of personnel. Let's consider the following scenario. The Wish-Well Card Company is expanding. Sales are up for a third straight year, and the physical size of the operation has doubled in the last two years. Wish-Well now has a staff consisting of an office manager, five artists, six secretaries, a national sales manager, three regional sales managers, twelve salesmen, two vice presidents, and one president. They also employ two graphic computer designers, a personnel manager, as well as an office boy, three shipping clerks, and a shipping manager. Their payroll consists of a total of forty employees.

The personnel manager, Henry Goforth, has heard all the arguments in favor of telecommuting. He wants to set up a telecommuting project for his company, but isn't sure where to start. There are several steps he will need to take; but, the first and most crucial step will be gaining the support of upper management. More telecommuting programs have failed due to lack of support by upper management than for any other single reason. The logic is simple. If the boss isn't sold on the idea, it doesn't have a fair chance of succeeding. At the first sign of trouble, the reins will be pulled in so tightly, Goforth may have trouble finding his desk!

Upper management must support and commit to the idea before it will fly. And they must be willing to do more than just support it. They must provide for it, nurture it, and take responsibility all along the way. Support comes in many forms. Merely rubber stamping the idea and offering limp approval won't get the job done. Management must commit three things to the program: time, money, and personnel. Telecommuting isn't a cheap proposition. It will, in the long run, save the company thousands of dollars, increase productivity, and provide a cutting advantage over the competition. However, like all innovative concepts, it comes with a price tag.

First, a commitment must be made to allocate the necessary cash to finance the operation. How much that will be will largely depend on how big a commitment the company is willing to make. But before Goforth can begin to count the cost, he must first decide which departments, and who in those departments, would be likely candidates for telecommuting positions. He must divide the workforce into five classifications: labor, clerical, sales, production, and management. By making this division, he will then able to categorize each employee into their own grouping. He can now begin his telecommuting program by department, rather than by employee.

It should be remembered that the definition for telecommuting included the statement "full or part-time." Not every employee can be a full time telecommuter. Some companies, such as The Travelers Group, of Hartford, Conn., require all telecommuters to work at least one day in the main office. Some agencies, such as the Department of Criminal Justice in California only allow their telecommuters to work at home two days a week. Others have employees who never come into the office. The amount of time spent telecommuting is directly related to the type of job and the type of employee doing that job.

Some detractors of telecommuting claim that any job which requires an employee to show up at the central office on a regular or even irregular basis, is in reality a duplication of efforts and a waste of money. The fact is that even if a person spent only 50 percent of his time telecommuting, then they are in effect representing at least a 50 percent savings in fuel consumption, parking facilities, and other space and energy related territorial usage. This being true, the two main problems Goforth has to face is not only who, but how often to allow an employee to telecommute.

Beginning a telecommuting program is often more a process of elimination than anything else. The first decision Goforth must make, once he has the support of management, is which departments will lend themselves most effectively to telecommuting. Manual labor is usually ruled out because those jobs are most generally performed on-site. Obviously, it would not be practical to try to ship boxes of greeting cards from the individual shipper's homes.

Clerical workers, however, are a different case. Some of Well-Wish's secretarial pool have job descriptions which really fall more toward the clerical side of secretarial work than the social side. Imputing orders, billing customers, and mailing statements can be done from an office at home as readily as it can be done from the main office. Highest on this priority list will be those workers whose primary function is data input.

Sales will be one of the easiest departments to convert to telecommuting. Most major industries today are accepting with greater enthusiasm the concept of telemarketing. Now with any such program, there are very few reasons why the sales person must be at a desk in the main office and literally dozens of reasons why he should not be. Today's business environment lends itself well to telemarketing. But as with all sales efforts, it is necessary for the buyer to be accessible to the seller and vice-versa. A sales representative who calls on customers across America via the telephone can better take advantage of time zones and geographical and logistical regions from an office based in his home than he can in a centrally located main office. The reason for this is that in telemarketing the salesman follows the sun as it crosses the four main time zones in the United States.

If the main office for Wish Well Card Company is located in Los Angeles, by the time a salesperson sits down to start calling accounts at 9:00 a.m. Pacific time, it is already noon on the East Coast. He or she cannot effectively begin to contact his or her East Coast customers until it is 1:00 p.m. Eastern time. This leaves him or her a window of only four hours to work the East Coast. But if that same salesperson begins his or her day at 6:30 from his or her home-based office a full two and a half hours before most of his or her competitors begin working, by noon he or she could begin working their Central Time or even Mountain Time customers. The advantage this would give the salesperson over his or her competitors is literally invaluable!

By the time his or her sales manager got to the office at 9:00 Pacific time, he or she would already have gotten in well over a fourth of his or her selling day. This would allow the order processing desk as well as the shipping department to gain hours on the shipping of orders. This, in turn, would give his or her customers the benefit of an extra day's head start on the receipt of his or her order. UPS deliveries from California to New York take six working days. The advantage of that extra day would mean that if a customer's ordering cycle was once every two weeks, Wish Well would be gaining an additional day every two weeks or an extra four selling cycles per year. Productivity would jump dramatically as a result of this head start.

But while it is one thing to have a commissioned salesman start the day at 6:30 a.m. from his or her home, it is an entirely different matter to try to get someone into a sales office at 6:30 in the morning. It would mean that he or she would have to leave his or her home at 5:45 just to drive to work. To leave home at 5:45 would necessitate getting out of bed no later than 4:45—something that most people would prefer not to do. The advantage to the telecommuting salesperson is obvious. He or she would finish his or her day by 3:30, having put in a full eight hours, allowing an hour for lunch. And when the salesperson's day is finished, he or she is *not* facing an hour and a half drive in rush hour traffic to return home.

## Implementation of the Plan

Obviously, the first place Goforth will begin his telecommuting efforts will be the sales department. And he won't stop there. Using a fax or a modem, the sales department will download their orders to a central processing computer system which will in turn begin to expedite orders as soon as they are fed into the system. Instead of orders sitting in a basket on a salesman's desk until the office boy comes by to collect them, they are electronically dispatched and the processing will begin within moments of the order being taken. Faster processing means faster shipping which means faster delivery, resulting in quicker return of receivables. The entire operation will benefit from this system, and within days, the cash flow of Wish Well will begin to improve. Using the formula already established for the decreased time frame which allowed an additional twenty-five days a year in which the order taking process has now gained, the net result to Wish Well is a decrease in the aging of receivables by 8 percent!

Goforth now turns his attention to the artists that design the cards his company sells. The work they now do in their office can be done at home, with a higher degree of efficiency. Once more, the time lost on the freeway is now spent creating new cards, expanding the line of goods the company can offer, and in turn, giving more product for the sales department to sell. As the sales department generates more sales, thanks in part to an increase in new product, the company will continue to grow.

In previous years, when Wish Well enjoyed a growth in business, adding more sales personnel and more artists to their payroll, it was necessary to increase the physical size of their office. They had previously been forced to lease more space or move their entire operation to bigger quarters. These growth adjustments normally result in a slow down if not a total stoppage of shipping and billing. Now, due to their implementation of a telecommuting program, not only do they not need to add additional space, but in many cases, they can actually decrease the size of the main office. The need for additional square footage decreases, and instead of increased expenses to offset increased profits, they begin to reap the benefits of less office space, less office equipment and furniture, and ultimately, less support personnel!

The money that would have previously been spent on non-sales related expenses can be channelled into better research and development, increased salaries, and bigger bonuses while still leaving a higher net profit margin. The employees are happy, the customers are happy, and the stockholders of Wish Well Card Corporation are overjoyed! Nobody loses, everybody wins!

# The Three Major Factors of a Telecommuting Project

These things are, of course, the pluses of telecommuting. There is a cost, however, and one which must be addressed. Before all these benefits can materialize, the company must do three things. First, it must determine that it is willing to commit to the program wholeheartedly. *This is not an experiment.* There are certain costs which will be incurred that cannot be fully recouped if the program fails. Additional mainframe equipment must be purchased, installed, and integrated into the already existing computer hardware. Terminals, modems, software, and fax machines will need be leased or purchased and, of course, additional phone lines will need be installed.

Secondly, the company must be absolutely certain that its present managers understand, endorse, and promote the telecommuting program. If a manager feels threatened by the sudden change in his or her job position, if he or she feels his usefulness to the corporation will somehow be diminished by the installation of this program, he or she will undermine Goforth's efforts. Managers must realize this move is not merely the scheme of one person hell-bent on revising the way Wish Well has done business for years; but rather, it has the full endorsement of the highest echelon of management. Managers must become managers in the truest sense of the word! They are now going to manage by objectives and results, not activity. They will be called upon to see that the program is utilized to its fullest extent and will need to apply every ounce of their managerial skills to insure the program is a success.

Thirdly, and this is the heart of any telecommuting program, management must hand pick which individuals will be chosen to participate in the project. Extensive efforts will need be expended to be sure that the participants realize that in exchange for the privilege of telecommuting, the company fully expects to see a marked increase in their productivity. To this end, it is incumbent on management to educate, encourage, and inform the prospective telecommuter of the realities and potential problems of telecommuting. This is best done by instituting several training sessions, either in groups or individually, which prepare the potential telecommuter for what he or she can expect once he or she begins working at home.

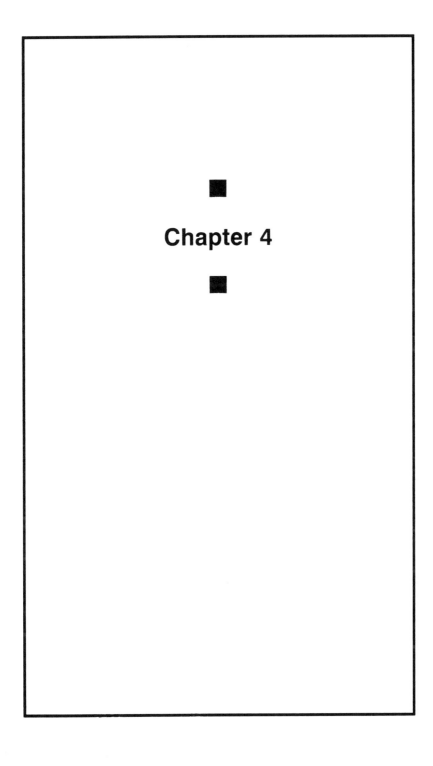

# Chapter 4

# Managing, Monitoring, and Motivating the New Telecommuter

## How to Manage the Telecommuter

As stated in the previous chapter, one of the most challenging aspects of telecommuting is the management of the telecommuter. There are several ways in which a telecommuter's performance can be measured, but they all boil down to one issue: production! Managing the off-site worker is a bit trickier than the worker that performs his tasks directly before your eyes; but in the long run, the telecommuter will most often be the more productive of the two.

## *Assignment of Production*

It is vital to the accomplishment of your department's goals that the work load is properly assigned and that the work assigned is completed in a timely and correct manner. Before your employee became a telecommuter, it was easy to take work which was not completed to your satisfaction, to drop it back on his or her desk, to tell him or her what was wrong, and to inform him or her how to correct the errors. This will now become a much more complicated procedure. To avoid this problem, be sure you assign the right person to the right job.

Stay in communication with your off-site worker. This does not mean constant communication! If you had an office-bound employee who consistently required supervision, in time you would replace that worker. Do not assume that merely because the telecommuter is out of sight, he must constantly stay within earshot. Establish early on just how often you expect to be in communication with the telecommuter. This communication can be by fax, phone, or personal contact.

If personal, face-to-face contact is necessary on a regular basis, arrange for the worker to come to you. It is not a good idea to go to the worker's home. There are three reasons for this. First, it places undue pressure on the worker. His job site is not only available for your inspection, but so is the rest of his domicile. This puts the worker in the position of being a host when you visit, instead of an employee. Secondly, it places the manager at a psychological disadvantage. He or she is not on his or her own "home" turf. This factor can present the supervisor in a less than an authoritative posture that the trappings of his or her own office often provide. Thirdly, it is not seemly, nor business-like, to visit an employee away from the business environment. In the case of male supervisors visiting female workers in the home, there is too great a possibility that at a later date, accusations, however unfounded, could be made concerning sexual harassment or impropriety. This doesn't even begin to take into account the personal problems that can arise out of such an arrangement in regard to the feelings of the telecommuter's significant other when he filters through his feelings about his wife's boss visiting her at home. These are not pleasant things to consider, but they are part of the reality of life and, as such, cannot be ignored.

This being the case, establish a day for in-office meetings with all telecommuters. Divide the number of telecommuters you have in each department by a factor of five and schedule an in-service day, one day each for one-fifth of your telecommuting staff. By doing this, you do not defeat one of the purposes for which the telecommuting program was originally established—the need to not have your entire staff in the office at the same time. Moreover, by spreading the meetings out over a period of an entire week, you are able to counsel each employee on a more personal basis, if not actually one-on-one.

## Establish Goals and Timetables

It will be mutually beneficial both to you and your employees if they are permitted to assist in long-range planning as well as establishing short-term goals for your department. In addition to fostering a team spirit, it also removes the premise many workers have that the boss expects too much, too soon. Encourage your telecommuters to participate in the planning sessions for your division and ask for their input into the setting of time frames.

Very little that is decided in planning sessions is carved in stone, but it should serve as a guide to help both the manager and the telecommuter work at a rate that will be conducive to the accomplishment of these pre-set goals. The use of timetables are broken down into three categories.

## Timetables

The timetable represents the overall amount of time allocated to a specific project. As an example, we will consider a textbook publisher. In order for a book to be ready in time for the schools to make a decision on whether or not they will by buying a particular textbook, the book must be in print by March 15 of the coming year. The book is assigned to a particular manager who is told the finished manuscript must be presented to the publisher by January 1 of that same year. The manager, in turn, assigns one of his telecommuting researchers to begin the initial research on the subject.

It is important that the telecommuter has a firm understanding that the book itself is expected to be at the publisher on January 1. While this date is well past the time his or her research must be completed, the very fact that the researcher is aware of the final due date will give the project a greater degree of urgency. Moreover, by being made aware of the overall timetable within which the project is expected to be completed, he or she is better able to see just where his or her contribution to the project fits into the overall effort.

Very often, telecommuters are deprived of a factor in their jobs which other workers take for granted. People working on an assembly line realize, by virtue of their proximity to their work, what their contribution to the finished product is. If a worker is responsible for soldering a wire to a contact, he or she is cognizant that if his or her wire is not in place before the next worker receives the work, the next worker cannot complete his or her job. It is the same way in the construction business. The worker who mixes mortar knows that bricks cannot be laid until the mortar is ready. In an information-based, white collar business, and especially when the added factor of telecommuting is considered into the equation, it is often possible for the worker to develop feelings that his or her work, while contributing the main effort of the organization, is merely a small cog in a large wheel. Allowing the telecommuter to see the big picture will result in having a better team player.

In sports, no coach would ever consider telling his players only part of a play. He wouldn't tell a quarterback to throw the ball to a certain place on the field without also telling the receiver that he will need to be at that place to catch the ball. He wouldn't leave the defensive players to figure out what to do when the ball is snapped anymore then he'd fail to tell the offensive linemen which men to intercept to insure the overall success of the play.

Yet, it is amazing how many department managers try to hold all their cards close to their chest feeding their employees only enough information to get through only one aspect of a project. A football coach with that attitude will never see a Super Bowl, and a company with that type of manager will never see the Fortune 500 list.

## Timeframes

The concept of timetables as opposed to timeframes is like a box within a box. The timetable is the overall allocation of time for any single project. A timeframe is that portion of time which is allocated to a particular job. For example, the researcher who contributes to the publishing project must understand that the book is due at the publisher on a specific date. However, it is imperitive that he or she understands that his or her research has its own specific due date.

If the book is to be ready for publication on the first day of January, then the manuscript must be completed at a significantly earlier date. Therefore, his or her research, which is a major component of that book, must be in at still an earlier date. Thus, the worker realizes that there are two dates with which he or she must contend. The former, the final completion date is not really his or her problem; but the latter, the date by which his or her research must be finished is a very real and a very integral part of his or her job. He or she is not a small cog, but rather an important gear. His or her work will be due and must be completed within a specific time-frame.

## *Timelines*

Timelines are where the manager of an off-site worker plays his greatest part. It is at this point that supervision becomes necessary. The preparation of a timeline is in reality nothing more than a written outline, broken down into specific events of when a project will be completed. For example, our researcher should submit a plan based on his or her best estimates of when certain milestones in his or her research will be accomplished. He or she should submit a week-by-week or, in some cases, a day-by-day analysis of how the work will be handled. If his or her research begins with point A and carries forward to point C, he or she should be able to state, with a certain degree of accuracy, at what point he or she will be working on point B.

This outline of his or her activities will serve two purposes. Obviously, it will allow the off-site worker to gauge his or her productivity and to adjust his or her work speed and output to match the pre-arranged timelines. *But of significant importance to the manager, it will allow him or her to manage by objective, not activity!* The manager will be able to ascertain whether the telecommuter is producing a sufficient quantity of work at a satisfactory pace. If the worker is producing as expected, then little of the manager's time will be wasted second guessing that employee. But if the worker is lagging behind his or her timeline, then a red flag goes up, alerting the manager to a potential problem. The manager is given, therefore, adequate time to correct the problem before it becomes a major issue.

It is through use of the timeline that the manager keeps his or her finger on the telecommuter's pulse. It is easier to correct a miscalculation in engineering before a railroad line is built than it is to correct laid tracks which miss each other by six inches. Timelines are somewhat a paradox: they allow the worker greater autonomy in performing his or her job while providing a supervisor greater control over how that job is done.

# Preparing the Telecommuter

There are certain changes which both the supervisor and the telecommuter will undergo as a result of this new work structure. As a telecommuter's manager, it is essential that you help prepare your employee for the things he or she will find once he or she actually begins the program.

## Change in Working Hours

It may be necessary to discuss with the off-site worker that a change in work habits is not an undesirable thing. So many workers have been beaten over the head with the same rules and regulations for so many years that a work ethic, uniquely American, has developed. Encourage your worker to find his own pace, his own peak times of production. He must realize that more latitude will now be tolerated in areas such as the time at which he or she begins and stops working, as well as how many hours he or she will work per week. But the telecommuter must also be made cognizant that this new-found freedom comes with a price tag—that is, your expectations for a higher degree of proficiency and a marked increase in productivity. *You must encourage your worker to use common sense.*

The exiting office worker should have a firm grasp about the realities of working at home. He should be warned about burnout. The one consistent factor which is most often cited about telecommuting burnout is that the isolation often becomes overwhelming. If a worker has spent the last twenty years of his life amidst the comradery and fellowship of a dozen or so workers and now suddenly finds himself alone in his home at ten in the morning every day, he may develop a serious case of lonliness or cabin fever.

Very few of us, in the midsts of a hectic day at the office have not wished for a nice quiet mountain retreat, a place where we could get our job done without the constant pressures and interruptions of that mad-house we call the office. But given that opportunity to be snowed into a mountain cabin for six weeks, most of us would be climbing the walls.

One method of preventing the burnout syndrome is to be sure that they don't become non-persons. Include the telecommuter in the same social functions that the office-bound worker enjoys. If telecommuters become a large enough sector of your employees, consider circulating a newsletter to the off-site workers. This is simple enough to do, and can be distributed via fax or modem to the workers at home. Include them, whenever possible, in the after hour social events also. One executive in San Diego, California, makes it a policy to meet with all his telecommuters over lunch one day a week. This allows an informal meeting of business associates and also helps prevent the feelings of isolation and separation which greatly contribute to burnout.

# Compensation and Benefits

Under no circumstances should a telecommuter be regarded as an employee not worthy of the same compensation and benefits that his or her fellow workers enjoy. Keep in mind, this worker is likely to be much more productive than the office bound, traditional worker. One of the greatest hidden fears of the off-site worker is that the company will employ the philosophy of "out of sight, out of mind." He or she is a telecommuter out of choice. He or she was given the option to work in the traditional mode, to venture into new territory, and to make new inroads into his or her profession or industry. *The telecommuter should never feel he is being penalized for this!*

The fact that the off-site worker stays at home to do his or her job does not mean that he or she is not entitled to the same rights and benefits enjoyed by his or her co-workers. This includes equal access to promotion. Having said this, it should be understood that within the reality of office politics, the chances a telecommuter will advance up the corporate ladder are, to a degree, somewhat less than the traditional worker with the same credentials. This fact should not be withheld from the office worker when he or she decides to begin a career of telecommuting. To offset this tendency, it would be prudent for a company with a telecommuting program to keep in mind that perhaps the person most qualified to supervise a telecommuting staff is the person who has been a telecommuter! This fact of life should not be dismissed when considering promotions from within the company.

# Coming Back to the Fold

Not every person who signs up for telecommuting will be successful in his or her attempt. It is important that before the employee leaves the office for the home work site, that he or she realizes in the event that home working doesn't prove successful, he or she may come back to the office, no grudges held. This is a very important safety net for the telecommuter. Without it, he or she may perceive the pressures of off-site employment to be much greater than they actually are. If the manager has done his or her job properly, the worker should leave the office for the home with the sure and certain knowledge that no bridges have been burned. He *or she can* come back. He or she *can* be reintegrated into the office work force.

Some workers do return to the office environment. Usually, however, if they are going to come back to the office, they do it within six to twelve weeks after leaving. Beyond that point, they will have successfully made the changeover and will have already begun to enjoy the luxury working at home affords them. But even this is not carved in stone. The birth of a child, the sudden burden of an aged parent moving in with an adult child, marriage or divorce, or any number of other unforeseen circumstances can and often will force the telecommuter to return to the daily freeway drive. If and when this happens, the company must be prepared to accept the worker back and to do so without any recriminations or comments.

# The Contract

After all the pros and cons have been presented to the telecommuting prospect and after all the rules and expectations have been explained, it is an excellent idea to put the substance of the discussions in writing. This document should be no longer than two pages. The document should state management's expectations as well as what support it intends to provide to the employee. It should outline the procedures for communication between the worker and the office. It is necessary to clarify who should be responsible for the initiation of ongoing communications. Because the essence of telecommuting is communication, it should be perfectly clear if it is management's or the worker's responsibility to maintain a regular schedule of communication.

In reality, this document is not a contract, per se, but rather a signed, informal agreement between both parties. It will enable both parties to avoid many problems and misunderstandings. And the document should state just that. It is a guideline, a mini-rule book, binding equally the company and the employee. It cannot begin to address all the problems which might arise, but it can lay out a procedure for dealing with situations and seeking the quickest possible solutions. State in the document the company's wishes to extend every possible aid and assistance to the employee and that, in turn, it fully expects the employee to perform to the best of his or her ability. This is no time to mince words. Spell out exactly what your company's expectations are and how you intend the employee to go about fulfilling them.

This would also be an excellent time to address the question of security and the problems attendant with having documentation taken off-site that would normally not be allowed out of an office. Include in the agreement that your company fully expects the off-site worker to maintain company files in a secure place and in such a manner as to afford them every reasonable protection.

Conclude this agreement with the proviso that at any time either party has the right to revoke the work-at-home concept and that assuming no wrong doing has occurred, the employee will be welcomed back to the office. This agreement is literally the ounce of protection worth pounds of cure!

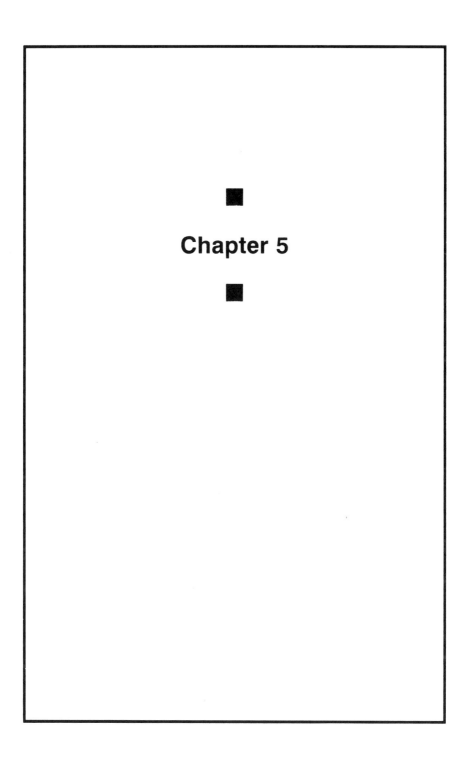

# Chapter 5

# Guides for Setting Successful Parameters for Telecommuters

**E**ight Guidelines Toward the Making of a Great Telecommuter Manager

There are a number of guidelines which, when followed by management, will make the telecommuter's job much more productive. These are not necessarily listed in order of importance, but they comprise the do's and don'ts of telecommuting supervision. They cover virtually every situation which will arise as your company moves its personnel into the newest concept for an effective deployment of its greatest assets, its employees.

(1) Show faith in your telecommuter. Don't expect him or her to know everything there is to know about this program. Stand ready to provide additional training and encouragement as it becomes necessary. To this end, the manager of a telecommuting program must be accessible to the off-site worker to a higher degree than was perhaps previously necessary when that same worker was employed within the confines of the main office. A telecommuter's manager should be prepared to spend extra time, at least in the beginning, with a new telecommuter. *He or she should know that the time will pay off handsomely in increased productivity, decreased bottom line expenses, and a deeper sense of accomplishment both on the manager's part and on the part of the telecommuter!*

(2) Always take the concept of telecommuting as a serious proposition. Its importance cannot be over emphasized. If management regards telecommuting as an experiment, as an oddity, then so too will its staff. Treat telecommuting as you would any other major shift in employment policy, and afford it the time and planning it requires.

(3) Organize and plan your objectives to the highest degree possible, but be prepared to change your expectations as your telecommuting program begins to take shape. Monitor the results much more closely than you monitor the players. If the

numbers are right, your company wins. If they are not, you lose. It's that simple. Chart and watch the progress, or lack thereof, of each project and each objective. Remember Lombardi's words of wisdom, "Winning isn't everything, it's the only thing." If the program is working, pour on more coal, find ways to make it even more productive. If it's not, find out why not, and correct it!

Telecommuting *does* work in almost every instance. If it isn't working for your company, trace the source of the problem and rectify the situation. This is the classic case of never throwing out the baby with the bath water! One or two strategically placed individuals, can result in a sabotaged program. If you suspect that is the case in your project, root them out and replace or convert those individuals.

(4) Do not ignore the staff that remains in the office. The temptation will be to focus all energies and efforts on the team that is working "away" from the office. This is an easy trap to fall prey to, and one which happens at some point in time to most managers as they watch, with justified pride, the results of the telecommuting staff. Remember, however, that no telecommuting project can be successful without the cooperation of those who stay behind, those who function as the liaison between the workers at home and the workers in the office.

It is easy to overlook the needs and

problems of the personnel left in the office. They too, need a period of adjustment. Francis Cardinal Spellman told a group of seminary students that while it is important to comfort the sick and the dying, it is equally important to comfort those that are alive and well! Do not pour all your efforts into understanding the problems of the newly created telecommuters. Working is a social activity as well as an economic one, and the work place, for many people, is the center around which their social life revolves. Have sympathy for the fact that those who remain in the office may well have lost their best friend, the person who occupied the next desk, the person with whom they have regularly eaten lunch, or had coffee. Now, suddenly, that person is not only gone, but in the eyes of the workers who remain in the office, they have gone to a better job.

(5)  Keep the team spirit alive by making sure there *is* a team! Include your off-site workers in as much of what goes on at the office as possible. Teleconferences are a brilliant use of time and resources. Help your workers find ways to increase their own efficiency. Don't wait for them to flounder; keep open the lines of communications so that minor problems don't have time to grow into major obstacles.

(6)  Remain flexible. Telecommuters need that degree of flexibility, and as their manager,

you must be sure they receive it. *Keep clearly at the forefront of your mind: objectives, not activity!* One of the worst mistakes a telecommuter's manager can make is to insist on hourly or semi-daily reports. This puts undue pressure on the worker who feels that he cannot now afford the luxury of a bad morning or a rough sales day. If a manager cannot trust his or her employee to do the job without constant supervision, then that employee has no business telecommuting—neither the manager nor the employee will benefit from the program.

(7) Set reasonable goals. A quota of any sort should contain two key elements. It should be set within parameters which both challenge the workers and allow the average worker to attain his or her goals. Make no mistake about this. Goals and quotas are absolutely essential to the success or failure of a telecommuting program. It must be stressed time and time again, the accomplishment of goals and objectives are the only means by which management can judge an employee's productivity. If goals are not set, the entire evaluation process becomes based on an assessment of activity, and anyone can look busy! Moreover, in the absence of obtainable goals, the employee cannot accurately measure his or her own performance. This lack could do more to harm the efforts of the entire department than any other single factor.

(8) The worst possible thing any telecommuter's manager can do is to ignore the telecommuter. Because of the distance involved, communications are vital to the success of the entire project. Give the problems of your telecommuters first priority when they call you. Keep in touch by fax, voice mail, E-mail, or pager. By whatever means you choose, keep yourself accessible to your off-site workers.

# Time as a Factor in Setting Up a Telecommuting Program

The establishment of a telecommuting program is a three step process: planning, recruiting, and implementation. Each step is vital to the program. However, some aspects of each segment will, by necessity, spill over into the others. This is to your benefit. For example, while planning the project, the key people who must be involved, that is, the personnel manager, the traffic manager, the data management department head, and of course, the various managers from the departments which will form the base from which telecommuting employees are recruited, will all have input and ideas as to who in their divisions will make the most likely candidates for telecommuters and, probably of equal importance, who would not. Therefore, while still in the planning stages, the recruitment process will already be started—albeit on an unofficial level. Likewise, while recruitment is underway, implementation will have already begun as a result of the planning stages during which decisions were made as to the quantities and types of hardware and software necessary to make the conversion. While it is possible to put the cart before the horse, it is not likely the three primary aspects of the implementation of your telecommuting program will become deprioritized.

# The Plan

As mentioned earlier, in the discussion of the Wish Well Card Company, it is necessary for strong upper management support—executives who can see the vision before telecommuting can become a reality. Step one of the planning phase is to select a group of executives, bringing in as many highly placed personnel as possible, and to begin to map out what departments are likely candidates for telecommuting, how much financial support the plan can expect and how limited, or in some cases unlimited, the company's interest is in bringing about such a project. Depending upon a number of variables, such as which departments are first targeted for initiation into telecommuting, the nature of those departments, the overall service or product the company produces as well as the extent to which the company is already enmeshed in technological equipment, both on-site and remote, and, of course, the size of the company, the costs for transforming one office bound employee into a telecommuter can range from as little as $400 to as much as $10,000.

To a large extent, that figure will rise in direct proportion to the potential telecommuter's degree of technical involvement. If the employee in question is a sales clerk, the outlay will be little more than an additional phone line, a computer entry terminal, and an extension line to the office. This could cost as little as $550, including the cost of delivery and installation. If, however, your company's first foray into the world of telecommuting will be a systems analyst concerned with the operational design and upkeep and modification of your data entry system, a much more elaborate selection of hardware will be necessary to maintain that off-site facility. While the initial cost will rise significantly as more hardware is installed in the off-site location, so too will the capability for greater productivity, and, ultimately, the greater bottomline profits. To cite a case in point, consider the case of a major insurance claims processor located in West Virginia. Each time they incurred a break down in their mainframe system, they would call in their systems analyst to set matters right. This would result in his being called at home, at all hours of the night, driving thirty-six miles to the location of the central office, many times in the most inclement of weather, only to sit down in front of a keyboard and spend ten minutes finding and correcting the problem. He would then drive back home and return to bed. He invested well over three hours, exposed himself to all degrees of hazards, both natural and man-made, to resolve a situation which really only required ten minutes at a keyboard. Once the company made the necessary installation of computer interfacing hardware and modems, at a cost of approximately $4500.00, this situation was rectified.

On the surface, it might have appeared cheaper to allow the analyst to drive to the central office than to provide the opportunity to resolve the problem from his home. But the issue really isn't the inconvenience the analyst would undergo each time the system broke down; the issue is really the loss of productivity the company incurred while the system was down! Although the analyst was inconvenienced as he made his trip to the central office, the company was incurring huge amounts of payroll cost for non-productive employees who could not enter data until the system was back on line. It also suffered a loss of computer time which could never be made up, unless the company was willing to pay overtime hours to compensate for system down time. In the case of companies which run three shifts, this overtime would have to come on weekends or holidays, during which time labor costs could be doubled or in some cases even tripled, just to make up lost computer time.

# Recruitment Procedures

Having established that a telecommuting plan is needed and desired by your company and having mapped out which departments will be targeted for the first phase of the plan, the next step is the recruitment of workers who wish to become telecommuters. Most companies do not have a problem finding workers who want to participate in this project, quite the contrary, most workers see this opportunity as a gift from God. The problem with recruitment, therefore, becomes not one of finding enough workers, but rather, finding the workers best suited for this style of work. There are no hard and fast rules by which an employee can be screened and determined to be fit for telecommuting. There are, however, criteria which can be applied to the worker to ascertain if, indeed, he or she possesses the potential for off-site employment.

Obviously, very high on this list of describable qualities will be the employee's desire to do this type of work. It is neither fair nor wise to force an employee to telecommute against his or her wishes. This would be analogous to a retailer hiring a person to sell jewelry and then putting them in the garden section of the store. If a person hired to sell jewelry wished to transfer to garden supplies, that's one thing; but to take a person who prefers to deal in one type of commodity and force him or her into a field in which he or she feels neither comfortable nor proficient, is the height of folly. Telecommuting *must* be voluntary!

Next, a telecommuter should be a highly organized worker. If his desk is in shambles at the office, imagine how it will look after the telecommuter has been home for two weeks. Organization is a skill which can be learned! Like any discipline, it comes easier to some people than others. Seek a telecommuter whose desk is organized, who has consistent, solid work habits, good time management skills, and who requires the least amount of supervision. This person is usually self-motivated and able to get himself or herself started without the glance or glare of his or her supervisor.

Watch also for the top performers, the workers who always seem to want more—more accounts, more clients, more responsibility. These are the types of a people who will thrive in the telecommuter's environment. They have always been restrained by corporate policy and inhibited by co-workers—left to their own devices, they would break all sales budgets, or input two weeks worth of data in a day and a half, or in one hour work through a programing problem that would have required three analysts an entire week to resolve, and still have time to keep their desks clear of clutter.

Also, look for the employee who doesn't seem to be comfortable around other people. This is not to say that the more anti-social an employee is, the better telecommuter he will make. But there is definitely a correlation between people who like to be left alone and good telecommuters. The shrinking violet in an office environment often becomes a blooming rose when protected by the friendly, non-threatening sur-roundings of his or her home.

One of the most important qualities a manager should consider when assembling his potential list of telecommuters is how well that individual knows his or her job. It makes absolutely no sense to move a worker who can barely bumble through his work day to a off-site situation where he will need to con-stantly call his supervisor for further instructions. The more knowledgeable the prospect is, the better his or her chances for success will be.

One final consideration should be the worker's home life. While this is not always an area of con-cern for the supervisor of an office bound worker, it is of profound importance when considering an em-ployee for a telecommuting position. Workers who have a strong history of good family relations, and who are steady in their marital relations, who have no outwardly manifestations of a troubled home life are more likely to be better telecommuters than one who often exhibits signs of marital discord or strife. The personal habits of an employee in regard to chemical dependencies, moral turpitude, and general social adjustments does not pose a serious problem to an employer if that employee can manage to keep those personal problems out of the office. But move that same worker to an environment such as his or her home, and if alcohol is a source of temptation to that worker, the telecommuting manager will soon be talking to an employee who is looped by eleven in the morning. This sort of determination is an extremely delicate issue, and the roads to litigation are fraught with employers who have acted hastily in determining if an individual is unfit for work due to a chemical dependency. The problem can only worsen when that employee is left unsupervised for days at a time.

In short, look for a sharply organized, well informed, hard working individual with a good home life who enjoys being on his or her own.

## Implementation

When the planning is finished and the employees are selected and the time has come to install the program, all that remains is the actual act of starting the project. The mechanics of setting up an off-site office, depending on the size of the corporation, will be done by either the telecommuter or by the company through either a contractor or, if the program is large enough, by a special division set within the corporate structure, such as engineering or a similar department, whose only purpose is the establishment of off-site work centers.

Depending on the size of the company, its dependency on electronic interfacing, and the type of job the telecommuter will be doing, the amount of equipment needed will vary. Some companies furnish the bare minimum needed to do the job. Anything extra becomes the burden of the telecommuter. Others furnish everything needed to outfit an office at home, from pens to desks and computers to fax machines.

Travelers Group of Hartford, Connecticut, provide their telecommuters with a complete work station. This includes a desk, a chair, a desk light, a two-drawer file cabinet, a personal computer stand, a personal computer, a telephone, an answering machine, a printer, and a modem. A data line is installed in the worker's home. In cases where it is deemed necessary, a fax machine and a copier is also furnished. In short, the home worker has everything he or she would need to do the same job if he or she were in his or her own office downtown.

Supplies are requisitioned through the same channels they would be if the worker was in the central office. Each full time telecommuter (defined by The Travelers as anyone working four days a week at home and one-half day a week in the office) can either bring in his or her work on a weekly basis or, if the need is more urgent, fax or send the information to the office over a data line via a modem. The time frame involved in the actual set-up of such an office takes The Travelers anywhere from two to six weeks to complete. The cost of the equipment, software, and installation will usually run in the neighborhood of $6000. This is no small amount, nor is it a small effort to assemble, deliver, and set up this much equipment. At present, The Travelers has two divisions from which telecommuters are drawn. These are the Managed Care/Employee Benefits Department and the Data Processing Department. They have telecommuters in five states with plans for further expansion of their program. Most companies operate on a much smaller scale with nowhere near the capital outlay that The Travelers Group invests. But regardless of the size of your company, the basic rule is the same. It is imperative that your home workers have the right tools to do the job. If it requires $6,000, then it would be foolish to spend less. The productivity of an off-site employee is the paramount issue when dealing with cost effective outlays for electronic equipment, as well as more traditional furniture. This is one aspect of business where the maxim, "penny-wise, pound-foolish" can be applied. Spend what it takes to get the program started and started right. To quote yet another British maxim, "Well begun is half done."

During the time the equipment is being installed in your off-site worker's home, spend some time going over the basic policy program that your company developed during the planning stage. It is during this time that the rules are laid out and contingencies covered.

Deciding how the off-site worker will be explained to customers and clients when they call the office is very important. Most companies are more comfortable with telling the callers the employee for whom they are looking is, "Not at his desk right now, but he will return shortly." Others tell the callers that,

"Mrs. Jones is telecommuting today. May I relay your call and have her get back in touch with you?"

Pacific Bell uses a different approach entirely. When a telecommuting employee receives an incoming call, the call is directed to the E-Mail center for that employee. The phone rings, and a message recorded by the employee begins. The recording has three main segments. First, it will identify the intended recipient. Secondly, it will inform the caller that the person called is not available (sometimes telling the caller when he or she will be available). Thirdly, it will inform the caller that if this is an emergency or if he or she needs to talk to someone immediately, he or she can dial another extension and speak to a different party—usually the assistant or that person's co-worker. Lastly, at the end of the message, there is time for the caller to identify himself and leave a message. A typical Voice Mail message sounds like this:

> "Hello, you've reached the voice mail box for Emma Watkins. I'm not at my desk right now. I check my box every hour. If you need to speak to me, you may leave a message at the end of this recording, and I'll call you back as soon as possible. If you need to speak to someone right now, you may call Laura Kenning at 555-1147. Thank you."

This approach to handling a call for a telecommuter is quite effective. At regular intervals, Ms. Watkins will call her voice mail box for her messages. If the caller needs someone, he or she can always call Ms. Kenning's number and talk to her. If he or she doesn't call Ms. Kenning, Ms. Watkins will call him back within the hour.

The implementation of a telecommuting program will at times, seem overwhelming. But remember that at some point each and every division or department in your company started from scratch. Sales started with one salesman, accounting with one accountant, and data entry with one clerk. Even Ford Motor Corporation started with one mechanic—albeit a genius—it still only had one! Keep communications open, stay fluid to new ideas and new concepts; above all, don't rush to judgement! Give special consideration to the philosophy that "Rome wasn't built in one day." Your telecommuting will require time as well.

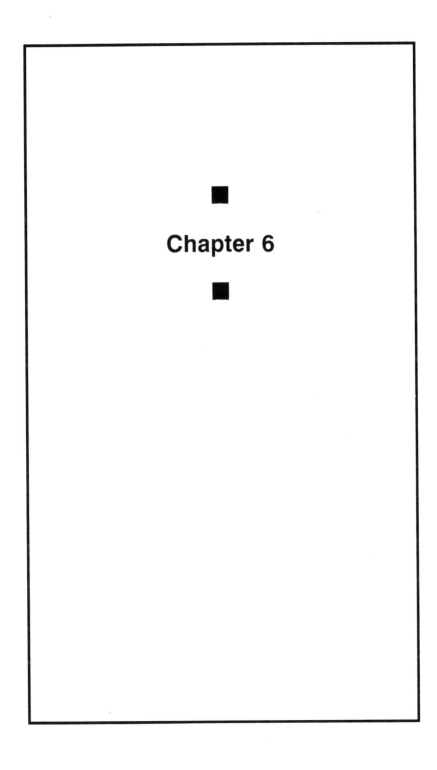

# Chapter 6

# Addressing the Various Factors of Liability Inherent in Telecommuting

## L iabilities Involved in Telecommuting

In any business venture, certain risks must be recognized. Telecommuting is no exception to this rule. There are five areas of liability which comprise the risk factors inherent in telecommuting.

### *Product Liability*

This is perhaps the least problematic of all the liability exposure your company will face when employing telecommuters on a regular basis. The risks run by an employee downloading incorrect data to the mainframe and that data becoming incorporated within the framework of a potentially dangerous product is rather remote, but it could happen. To safeguard your company, a simple product liability policy may be purchased from almost any insurance company which will afford your firm cheap and sufficient coverage to protect your venture from any such actions as wrongful death or reckless endangerment arising from the calculations and input of faulty information.

The problems of product liability are further diminished when the work done by one employee is checked by a second or even a third worker. This allows a fresh eye to examine the product design for possible engineering flaws and, at the same time, provide an opportunity to perhaps enlarge or expand on an existing or new product. In short, product liability is the least of your worries at this point in the implementation of your telecommuting program. However, other types of liability do exist, some of which cannot be insured against.

# Employee Liability

Employee liability enters the equations when the work done by the employee is allowed to be downloaded directly into the mainframe without first having proper safeguards installed. Actions such as entering a wrong code, or crediting a wrong account for deposits, or payments could, if not rectified quickly, result in a substantial loss to the corporation. For example, if a telecommuting accountant enters a code instructing the accounts payable computer to issue a check to an insurance company for less than the full amount of a premium due on the corporate jet and that jet crashes into a shopping center two days after the grace period has expired on the policy, the insurance company is no longer responsible for the financial loss incurred by the crash. That error made by the telecommuting employee could initially cost the corporation millions of dollars.

One might argue that such an occurrence could have taken place at the central office, and the fact that the accountant was working from home was not a significant factor in the error. While this is a valid argument, it must be conceded that in an office environment, such an underpayment might well have been spotted by a data entry clerk, a secretary, or even another accountant. By working alone, perhaps at night, perhaps without proper rest or under the influence of a mind altering chemical such as alcohol or narcotics, the accountant increased his chances of making such a major miscalculation.

There are remedies to this sort of problem, but these remedies take time to implement, and that implementation should take place as soon as practical. For example, a program can be written instructing the payroll department's computer to write no check over a certain amount without first verifying the authenticity of that check. It could also be instructed that no check be automatically issued to a party to which a previous check had been issued if the new check was more than 15 percent greater than the largest check ever issued to that party. Likewise, billing errors could be held to a minimum using the same type of limit-alert procedures.

If an hourly employee earning minimum wage were to find a check in his weekly pay envelope drawn in the amount of $55,400 instead of $55.40, that employee would probably set a speed record getting to the bank. Such errors have occurred before, and they will again. Newspaper stories abound with tales of little old ladies who receive gas bills for $140,900, or telephone bills in excess of a $250,000. These miscalculations are quickly rectified, of course, but not before causing a great deal of bad publicity for the utility involved.

Again, it would be unfair to say that telecommuting was responsible for these or other mis-billings. The point is that if such problems can occur in an office environment, then they can also, and may more likely, occur in a telecommuting situation. The remedy is of course a mixture of proper care on the part of the employee, proper supervision on the part of the manager, and proper safeguards in place all along the computer trail.

### Property Liability

Property liability extends beyond the damage done to the equipment the company has lent out for the employees' use. It can be extended to include the home of not only the worker, but the homes of those living in close proximity to him.

The XYZ company decided to allow one of its data processors to become a telecommuter. All the employee had to do was take home the terminal, connect it to the modem, the telephone line, and an electrical outlet. She plugged in the printer, the video display screen, the fax machine, the answering machine, the calculator, the lamp, the radio, the electric pencil sharpener, and a small fan. Into one outlet which had twenty extension cords, the telecommuter plugged in 2900 amps. Now, she was ready to do business. She turned on all the appliances, went to the kitchen to get a cup of coffee, and by the time she returned, the wall was already on fire and, within minutes, the house was a smoking piece of charcoal.

Whose fault was this? Who's going to foot the bill for this one? Most jurisdictions would find the company at fault, not because it instructed the telecommuter to overload the circuitry of her home, but because it was negligent in not overseeing that the installation of the computer (and all its attendant hardware) was done in a safe and prudent manner. In a case with exactly this set of circumstances, a jury in New York awarded the telecommuter and various other individuals living in the same apartment building, a settlement in excess of 6 million dollars. Upon appeal, the case was settled for 3.2 million. Fortunately, the company was adequately insured to cover such a loss. But the point is this: if the company had installed the equipment itself, if it had taken the extra step to see that everything was done properly and safely, the fire would never have happened, and the whole incident would have been prevented. The loss of productive time which should have been spent making sure the company fulfilled its first obligation—that is, making a profit for its stockholders—cannot be calculated. Hundreds of man hours were lost as the company conferred with its insurance company, haggled with adjusters, and evaded newspeople. By paying a single technician less than a hundred dollars, the whole mess could have been avoided.

Any company can significantly reduce its risk of such a scenario unfolding for it if it takes very simple precautions. See that equipment installed in the telecommuter's home is properly installed. See that all installations meet or exceed the electrical code requirements for such installations. Most of all, exercise a bit of common sense. Don't hold the dime so close to your eye that you cannot see the dollar. Do the job right the first time!

### Tax Liability

Tax advantages for firms which employ telecommuters abound. The problem is not in finding tax write-offs, but rather exercising caution so that your company does not fall into the traps, in which many others have already found themselves. Many corporations have sought to save tax dollars by treating their telecommuters as contract labor. The concept of contract labor is a brilliant idea, and if properly used, it can save a corporation or a small business a great deal of capital outlay. It is a given that somewhere between 30 and 40 percent of corporate payroll is comprised of "benefits" or "perks." Group insurance, sick days, paid holidays, car allowances, even company cars, all contribute to inflating the worker's total compensation package. Add to this a vast array of taxes (some hidden, some not) and the cost for each employee becomes higher and higher. No one could fault a company for trying to shift some of these expenses off their books and onto the backs of the workers. But herein lies the trap.

There is not clear cut definition of what makes a person an employee, what constitutes a free-lance operator, or a self-employed individual. There are as many different criteria as there are examples to cite. While there are numerous ways to ascertain whether or not an individual is an employee or an independent contractor, there are certain minimum criteria which must be met before the company can hope to convince the various labor unions and taxing entities that they are, indeed, dealing with a bonafide independent contractor.

1) An independent contractor sets his or her own hours. An employer cannot require them to work a certain number of hours, nor can the independent contractor be compelled to work within a specified time frame. The exception to this is that a contracting employer may have reasonable business expectations, and if those expectations can be fulfilled only by the independent worker performing the contracted task during certain hours, then those hours can be specified. For example: XYZ company imports and sells leather coats to retailers. XYZ pays its salespeople on a commission basis only. It maintains that these salespeople are contract employees; as such they are not eligible for company benefits. XYZ does require, however, that the salespeople actively make calls on the trade between the hours of ten in the morning and four in the afternoon.

This does not violate the concept of telling a contract employee when to work. Common sense would dictate that in order for the contractor to properly perform on the contract, he or she must call on the trade during the hours when he or she would be more likely to actually sell the product. It would be highly unlikely that any buyer would be receptive to a sales call at two in the morning; therefore, it is not outside the realm of reason to expect a salesperson, regardless of his or her status as independent or company employee, to make his or her sales calls during the daytime hours.

Conversely, if the contractor is hired to input data into the company's computer system and that data can be inputed anytime within a twenty-four hour time frame, then the company cannot tell the independent contractor when to input that data, as long as the data is entered within a time frame which will allow the company access to that information on a timely basis.

2) An independent contractor operates from his or her own office or work place. He or she is responsible for his or her own equipment, tools, and overhead expense. The employer may, as a matter of convenience to all parties involved, provide the contracting individual with a work space and tools of the trade, providing that some sort of arrangement is made to compensate the company for the use of that space or tools. Many

telecommuters lease the terminal from which they perform their work from the company for whom they do their work. This is not the same as providing a terminal for the contractor's use; but rather, places the company in the position of being a leasing agent which, in and of itself, opens an entirely new avenue of tax advantages through depreciation of equipment and potential "paper" losses which occur when the leased equipment brings in less revenue than it costs to purchase and maintain.

3)  The employer may not restrict the business activities of the contractor except in regard to possible conflict of interests, and to this end, each employer must decide what constitutes a conflict of interest. In the case of an independent insurance agent, it is obvious that agent will represent many different companies. To force that agent to represent only one company would, in effect, make that person an agent for that one company, thereby making him or her an employee, not an independent contractor. But if that same agent sells not only life insurance for the ABC Life Insurance Corporation, but also wishes to sell liability coverage for the DFG Insurance Corporation, then no restrictions may be placed upon that agent in regard to how many different types of insurance he or she wishes to broker.

As an employing corporation, however, the ABC Life Insurance Company may stipulate that a criteria for brokering its product is that the broker may not handle the product of a viable competitor. He or she may handle other life insurance companies, but none that are on a par with the ABC company.

4)   Independent contractors may provide their services or products to any person they wish without regard to company policy concerning pre-specified criteria as to the type of business or individuals the company may wish to seek as clients. The company does retain the final right of acceptance. Through its pre-specified criteria, it may well reject an offer to do business with another entity based on considerations such as credit worthiness, area saturation of its product, or the type of entity seeking to buy its services or products.

If, for example, the Wiggins Belt Company didn't wish to sell their belts to a discount clothing store and maintained a company policy of selling only to specialty shops for the specific purpose of maintaining the image of its product, it would be within its rights to refuse an order taken by its independent contractor to supply its product to the Cheap-Way Bargain Basement Blow Out Mart Corporation. (The basis of this comparison is strictly for the assessment of what constitutes an independent contractor and does not proport to be the final word on the ethics or civil liabilities which may follow on the heels of any company wishing to initiate such an elitist policy.)

5) All independent contractors must be treated the same, but not all independent contractors must be equally compensated. The very essence of being an independent contractor lies in the contractee's ability to negotiate the best possible deal for him- or herself or for his or her company. If each contractee was held to the same rate of compensation as all others, there would be no incentive for that contractee to provide exceptional service or sales for the contractor. Therefore, it is both advisable and desirable that each contractor promote his or her own rate of compensation based on the degree of professionalism which that individual or individual's company is able to bring to the corporate bargaining table.

## Security Liability

One of the most frequently raised objections to telecommuting is the question of security with regard to company business and classified corporate information. The irony of this is that the advent of telecommuting did not, in and of itself, increase the likelihood of such an occurrence; but, the technical advances which made the entire concept of telecommuting viable, have opened the floodgates of industrial espionage to a degree never before imagined.

The fact is any employee with almost any firm has access to enough information within his or her daily grasp to undermine any corporate operation. In the beginning of the computer age, information was stored on disks the size of garbage can lids and printouts were done on paper wide enough to carpet a small room. Stored information could not be retrieved without first building a computer the size of a house. There was little likelihood that anyone would try to actually steal data in raw form. As the computer technology continued to advance, the physical size became smaller and smaller. Now, with the use of the three and one-half inch disk, the most sophisticated level of information can be placed inside a man's shirt pocket or a woman's change purse. In short, if an employee wants to take home the company's customer list or its marketing plans for the next six months, most could.

In truth, the problem of data security does not lie with armed security guards or sleuthful corporate executives, but rather with the personnel office. If the right caliber of people are hired initially and if the right type of management is in place, the chances for corporate espionage is drastically reduced. With this in mind, consider that the problem is not one of how to keep the data safely in the office, but rather, how to keep the wrong people from getting their hands on what your company considers private information.

Unfortunately, as technology advances, so does the means for defeating the security attendant to electronic files. Many times, the matter of security often is not considered until the damage is done. As recent incidents have indicated, hackers, those people who illegally enter the data base of both private and public concerns, often operate with impunity. The reality of the matter is that corporations often have more to fear from outside raids on their data banks than from internal leakage.

There is an area of concern, however, in regard to telecommuters and the security of the work they do. It is often much easier to break into a private residence than it is an office. To that end, some considerations should be given to be sure your telecommuters take at least the most obvious steps to secure any documentation that they may access. Often it is not the information which the telecommuter is working on which is of interest to an industrial spy, but rather the terminal by which the trusted telecommuter can gain access to the company's mainframe. There are certain steps which can be taken to help prevent a successful penetration of your corporate security.

Each telecommuter should be assigned an access code that allows only him or her access to the central computer. Impress on the employee that this code is restricted and, as such, no one should have knowledge of the code or the sequence required to place the code in use. Each code should be constructed in a manner insuring that the telecommuter would have no need to write down the access number; yet, it should be memorable. Avoid using codes which are constructed of such numbers as the telecommuters birth date, social security number, or driver's licence. These numbers are obviously the most likely to be readily available to any person familiar enough with the telecommuter to have access to his or her machine.

One company that uses telecommuters on an extremely heavy basis decided early on to allow the telecommuter to pick his own code using a combination of his mother's maiden initials combined with the birth date of either his father, mother, or any grandparent. This resulted in a code which was intensely personal, yet easy to remember. A casual hacker could not have known the components of the code, let alone how they were selected!

But no telephone line is immune from bugging. If your company deals in sensitive information, there are some common sense steps you can take to lessen the risks of leaks or exposure.

First, make sure your telecommuter understands the fact that he or she is dealing with material which needs to be safeguarded. A Silicone Valley electronics development company, who for obvious reasons does not wish to be identified by name, conducts an exit seminar for its new telecommuters that is heavily laced with the concerns and problems of home security. They open the session with a simple chat. The telecommuting candidate is asked by the interviewer, almost absent mindedly, "Is today Monday?" Now, the interviewer already knows that it is Tuesday, not Monday. The purpose of this question is to show the new telecommuter how much information we all give away, each day, for free. Almost to the person, each respondent will answer, "No, it's Tuesday."

## *STOP!*

What's wrong with that answer? The question wasn't "What day is this?" The question was, "Is today Monday?" By answering with more information than was requested, the telecommuter gave a perfect example of how information can be leaked unintentionally. Now this particular question has little significance in the day to day scheme of things, but it serves to illustrate to the telecommuter the need to be on guard, especially with acquaintances and friends. How they discuss what they do and where they do it can become a serious breech of security. Remember the World War II motto, "Loose lips, sink ships!"

There is no absolute iron-clad way to protect data that is being accessed from your mainframe. One thing that can be done, however, is to keep security a high priority factor in your dealings with your telecommuters and your installers. Remain vigilant and alert. Keep your employee's attention focused on the need for security awareness.

There are many ways to increase security in the home and thereby decrease the risks of leakage.

1) Install a perimeter audio alarm device. This sort of installation is not expensive to purchase, is easy to install, and is relatively maintenance free. The purpose of this device is to alert the people living in and near the telecommuting site that an intruder has entered the area in which the computer hard-

ware is used. This is a good idea, not only for data security, but also because computer hardware is expensive and has, in recent years, become more of a target for home burglars. The theft of the computer is not only a problem for the telecommuter, but it will also slow down whatever production his or her company is expecting of him or her. Replacing a stolen computer is not like replacing a car stereo or a television. The new machine will need to be installed, programed, and introduced to the mainframe all over again. This is truly a case of an ounce of prevention being worth a pound of cure.

2) Instruct your telecommuters to turn off their terminals if they are going to leave the house, even for a short trip. There is no point in going to the trouble and expense of installing an access code if the machine is going to be left on when no one is home. This would be analogous to installing an elaborate burglar alarm and then leaving the front door wide open.

3) Warn your workers to position their video display screens (VDS) so they are not visible to people sitting in a car across the street with a pair of high power binoculars. This is not far-fetched. Robert Hotch, an industrial espionage expert, claims that it is possible to glean a great deal of information from such a simple surveillance operation. He claims to have photographed entire market-

ing reports as they came across the screen of a telecommuter—reports which included customer price codes, price increases and decreases, as well as customer lists and future marketing plans. All of this data was gathered from an automobile parked across the street from the workers' home!

4) Be sure your employee is mindful that any printouts he generates and then discards are of critical importance. The supreme court has ruled that once garbage is put out for the sanitation department to pick up, it becomes fair game for any governmental agency or private concern. If you do not provide your telecommuter with a paper shredder to dispose of old printouts, then institute a policy of having him bring old printouts into the office for disposal.

5) Remind your telecommuters to maintain some common sense approaches to security—keep doors and windows locked and pay attention to strange vehicles in the neighborhood. Be sure that any representatives from local utility companies have proper identification before being admitted into the home. Moreover, be sure that if a person knocks on the telecommuter's door and claims he or she is with your company and has been sent to make a modification to his or her hardware, that the worker is either known to the telecommuter or that the individual's identification is checked through the main office.

6) Security of data is not as easy to accomplish as the security of the hardware. If it is possible, try to see that the telecommuter works in an area of his home that can be closed and locked. One company on the west coast goes a step further. They provide the telecommuters with a dead bolt lock to secure their work area when they are not home. It costs about $50, installation included. There is no way to estimate how much such a lock can save! Security is a common sense problem, and common sense problems usually have common sense answers. If you see that your telecommuter is aware of the dangers inherent in this type of industrial espionage, many of the problems will cure themselves.

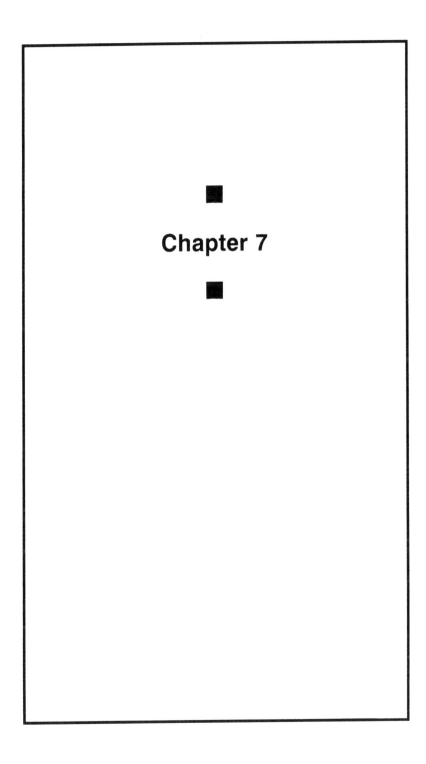

# Chapter 7

# Telecommuting as It Applies to Government and Semi-Public Entities

## San Diego County Telecommuting Program

Some telecommuting programs are born out of an organization's desire to remain in the forefront of the newest trends. Some come out of basic needs for which there is no other viable solution. And some come from a hybrid of need and desire. This was the case in the County of San Diego. On June 5, 1990, the voters of California enacted Proposition 111, known as the *"Traffic Congestion Relief and Spending Limitation Act of 1990."* The proposition was a mixed bag of reforms and censures. But the main thrust of the legislation was that something would need to be done if the State of California was not soon to become one giant snarl of traffic congestion moving at three miles an hour during most of the day. The Act required the implementation of a traffic congestion relief program. It required a congestion management plan able to identify service levels, manage transportation demands, and simultaneously address the problems of various congestion related issues such as fuel consumption, road way taxes, and trip reductions.

If San Diego County was to continue to share in the proceeds from the gas tax revenues which were part and parcel of this proposition, it must first qualify for such participation by instituting a congestion relief plan. It followed, therefore, that one of the aspects of this plan would be a county-wide implementation of some sort of telecommuting program.

One of the elements tending to make telecommuting such a viable option for state and local governments, is that the business of most governmental agencies is the gathering and distribution of information. For this purpose, many times all that is needed is a telephone and a personal computer terminal. Telecommuting and governmental activities are a match made in heaven. It was necessary for the county to identify the departments which were most easily converted to a telecommuting program.

By the time Proposition 111 came into existence in June of 1990, the County of San Diego had already begun their telecommuting program. On February 13, four months before they were obligated to do so, the County of San Diego started their program with fourteen telecommuters and their supervisors. It was determined that the best way to start this program would be with a test project. The Department of Public Works was selected for the project's first department.

The DPW was an excellent choice for the new test program because so much of their work is in the area of information classification and exchange. Because the very nature of telecommuting is the exchange of information, a department which exists on this type of work would be the most likely to benefit from such an experiment. Employee classes included in the study ranged from EDP System Analysts to the office of the Assistant Land Surveyor. The participants were all volunteers and included both single and married people, both with and without children living at home. Each volunteer was carefully screened before being selected for this project. The study was concluded and among the findings were:

1) Employee morale and motivation was greatly enhanced.

2) Productivity among the telecommuting participants increased by as much as 40 percent in some cases.

3) Employees reported a marked decrease in stress levels for both their job and the daily commute between home and work.

4) The four-month study saved more than 3,300 vehicle miles by the employee partici-

pants not having to make a trip into work on their respective telecommuting days.

5) A tightly monitored telecommuting program potentially could save the county about $1,440 per year in office space costs for every person that telecommutes two or more days per week.

## Setting Up the Program

One of the first myths the county had to overcome was the public's perception that, at best, governmental employees are not hard workers. The county took a three-prong attack on this assertion. First, extensive use of the local media was used to help educate the public to the need and practicality of this alternative work form. Secondly, to insure that the county would not be embarrassed by any of the workers selected for the program, it carefully screened all volunteers, selecting only those whose work record was exemplary and whose absentee rate was almost nonexistent. By choosing workers with the best work record, San Diego County bypassed the possibility that they would end up with slackards or workers merely looking for a way not to do their jobs while still drawing a pay check. Thirdly, the county spent many hours re-training their supervisory personnel toward the concepts of managing by objective, not activity. They emphasized productivity, completion of work assignments, deadline restrictions, and personal accountability. Using these three approaches, the first hurdle, that of pre-publicity, was overcome before it had a chance to become a stumbling block to the progress of the program.

## The Screening Process

Before an employee was accepted into this voluntary program, each underwent rigorous scrutiny designed to fit the best candidates to the positions they sought. This screening was aided by the use of a supervisor's evaluation report, called an *Employee Characteristic Assessment,* and by a participant's survey, called a *Telecommuting Screening,* as well as a third survey called, *The Pre-Pilot Attitudinal Survey.*

## The Employee Characteristic Assessment

The purpose of this survey was to determine if an employee fit the basic profile of a telecommuter. Among the questions it sought to answer were: (1) Is this candidate a self-starter? Has he or she exhibited in the past, under direct supervision, the ability to work at his or her own pace without the watchful eye of a supervisor? Has he or she consistently produced significant quantities of work, without being prodded by his or her supervisors? (2) Is this candidate able to produce, with or without constant instructions, a volume of work which is measurable on some scale? (3) Does this candidate demonstrate a true and real commitment to his or her work and to his or her career? (4) Does this candidate realize that the opportunity to telecommute is a privilege—one that must be never be considered a right— and is he or she able to recognize the significance of this privilege?

This survey consisted of a group of questions intended to reveal the degree of competency and maturity level of the potential telecommuter. The candidate was given a series of multiple choice questions. The first part of the survey dealt with general information and was concerned primarily with how conversant the candidate was with regard to telecommuting and how realistic his or her individual goals were. The second part of the survey was posed in such a way as the respondent would answer by checking the appropriate box marked either [H] heavy, [M] medium, or [L] low. The survey, listed below, was given to any person interested in participating in the pilot program.

I.   General Information

1.   Have you ever telecommuted before?

_____ a.   Yes, frequently

_____ b.   No

_____ c.   Occasionally

2.   How often do you expect to telecommute?

_____ a.   One day every two weeks

_____ b.   One day a week

_____ c.   Two days a week

_____ d.   Three days a week

_____ e.   Four days a week

_____ f.   Occasionally, for a project

_____ g.   Other (please specify)

3.   What is the business problem to be addressed by telecommuting?

_____ a.   Recruiting/retention

_____ b.   Office space

_____ c.   Productivity

_____ d.   Absenteeism

_____ e.   Regulation/ordinance compliance

_____ f.   Emergency preparedness

_____ g.   Other (please specify)

II.   The following groups of characteristics relate to yourself, your work, and your manager. Please rate each characteristic as high, medium, or low by placing a check mark in the appropriate space.

| Employee Characteristics | H | M | L |
|---|---|---|---|
| Need for supervision, frequent feedback | [ ] | [ ] | [ ] |
| Organization and planning skills | [ ] | [ ] | [ ] |
| Self-starting | [ ] | [ ] | [ ] |
| Need of colleagues input | [ ] | [ ] | [ ] |

Motivation derived from promotion
   possibility                                    [ ] [ ] [ ]

Discipline regarding work                          [ ] [ ] [ ]

Discipline regarding personal issues
   (visiting with neighbors, watching
   television, etc.)                              [ ] [ ] [ ]

Desire/need for social interaction                 [ ] [ ] [ ]

Level of experience                                [ ] [ ] [ ]

Potential friction at home while working  [ ] [ ] [ ]

**Work Characteristics**

Amount of face-to-face interaction
   required                                       [ ] [ ] [ ]

Ability to organize face-to-face inter-
   action into scheduled time period              [ ] [ ] [ ]

Telephone interaction required                     [ ] [ ] [ ]

Computer interaction required                      [ ] [ ] [ ]

Amount of assessing performance via
   quantitative measures (number of
   reports, reviewed, written, etc.)              [ ] [ ] [ ]

Amount of clear cut objectives
established                                         [ ] [ ] [ ]

Ability to control and schedule work.              [ ] [ ] [ ]

Amount of in-office reference material
   needed to perform your job.                    [ ] [ ] [ ]

Required level of security for data                [ ] [ ] [ ]

## The Telecommuter Screening Survey

This survey was taken by supervisors and managerial personnel to help ascertain their level of commitment to the concept of telecommuting. The primary purpose of this survey, however, was to determine how the county's telecommuting program could be best structured and to help determine which departments could be brought into the pilot program as well as which could not. This survey is broken down into two parts: the first is presented in the form of a question and answer; the second is multiple choice, using the H, M, L designation previously used in the screening of the telecommuting candidate. The basic difference between the two surveys is that this survey was used to determine which managers and department heads were most receptive to the idea of telecommuting and which were not.

## Supervisor Screening Survey

I.   General Information

1.   How many employees under your direct supervision will be telecommuting? _____

2.   Have your employees telecommuted before?

_____ a.   Yes, frequently

_____ b.   No

_____ c.   Occasionally

3.   How often will your employees be telecommuting?

_____ a.   One day every two weeks

_____ b.   One day a week

_____ c.   Two days a week

_____ d.   Three days a week

_____ e.   Four days a week

_____ f.   Occasionally, for a project

_____ g.   Other (please specify)

4.  What is the business problem to be addressed by telecommuting?

_____ a.   Recruiting/retention

_____ b.   Office space

_____ c.   Productivity

_____ d.   Absenteeism

_____ e.   Regulation/ordinance compliance

_____ f.   Emergency preparedness

_____ g.   Other (please specify)

5.  What work will they do while telecommuting?
(Check all that apply.)

[  ] Administrative work

[  ] Analysis

[  ] Auditing reports

[  ] Batch work

[ ] Calculating

[ ] Computer conferencing

[ ] Conducting business by telephone

[ ] Contract preparation/monitoring

[ ] Data analysis

[ ] Data entry

[ ] Data manipulation

[ ] Data processing

[ ] Data programing

[ ] Dictating

[ ] Field visits

[ ] Maintaining data bases

[ ] Meeting with clients

[ ] Planning

[ ] Project oriented work/management

[ ] Reading

[ ] Record keeping

[ ] Research

[ ] Sending/receiving electronic mail

[ ] Spreadsheet analysis

[ ] Support activities

[ ] Thinking

[ ] Typing

[ ] Word processing

[ ] Writing

[ ] Other (please specify)

6.  What equipment/services do your employees need to successfully telecommute? (check all that apply.)

Need Have

____ ____  Additional phone line

____ ____  Answering machine

____ ____  Bookcase

____ ____  Calling card

____ ____  Computer/terminal

____ ____  Desk

____ ____  Facsimile machine

____ ____  File cabinet

____ ____  Modem

____ ____  Pocket pager

____ ____  Printer

____ ____  Software

____ ____  Typewriter

____ ____  Voice mail

____ ____  Other (please specify)

## Work Characteristics

|  | H | M | L |
|---|---|---|---|
| Amount of face-to-face interaction required | [ ] | [ ] | [ ] |
| Ability to organize face-to-face interaction into scheduled time period | [ ] | [ ] | [ ] |
| Telephone interaction required | [ ] | [ ] | [ ] |
| Computer interaction required | [ ] | [ ] | [ ] |
| Amount of assessing performance via quantitative measures (number of reports, reviewed, written, etc.) | [ ] | [ ] | [ ] |
| Amount of clear cut objectives established | [ ] | [ ] | [ ] |
| Ability to control and schedule work | [ ] | [ ] | [ ] |
| Amount of in-office reference material needed to perform your job | [ ] | [ ] | [ ] |
| Required level of security for data | [ ] | [ ] | [ ] |

## Manager Characteristics

| | | | |
|---|---|---|---|
| Positive attitude in regard to the concept of telecommuting | [ ] | [ ] | [ ] |
| Trusts employee's ability to successfully telecommute | [ ] | [ ] | [ ] |
| Organization and planning skills | [ ] | [ ] | [ ] |

Ability to establish clear objectives          [ ] [ ] [ ]

Provides feedback regularly          [ ] [ ] [ ]

Flexibility          [ ] [ ] [ ]

Ability to communicate with others          [ ] [ ] [ ]

Product-oriented (results) rather than
   activity-oriented (process)          [ ] [ ] [ ]

## The Pre-Pilot Attitudinal Survey

The pre-pilot attitudinal survey was administered to both supervisory personnel and telecommuting candidates. The purpose of this final survey was to assess the attitudes and expectations of management and labor toward telecommuting. The same set of questions were given to the participants of the project at the end of the pilot program to see if the attitudes toward telecommuting had remained the same, had improved, or had deteriorated. The length of time elapsed in the San Diego project was one year. Elapsed time may vary, but certainly no less than a six month test program should be considered.

## Management's Survey

The following survey has been designed to assess your attitudes toward and expectations from your staff's participation in the test program. You will be asked to complete a similar survey at the end of the project to determine how your attitudes have changed. All responses are confidential and will be used for statistical purposes only.

I.    General Information

1.    _____    How many people do you supervise?

2.    _____    How many of the people you supervise will be telecommunicating?

3.          Approximately, how often do you expect your staff to be telecommunicating?
(Check one only)

_____    It will vary from person to person

_____    Once every two weeks

_____    Once a week

_____    Two days a week

_____    Three days a week

_____    Other (please specify)

4.    What kinds of work will they do while telecommuting? (Check as many as apply.)

[ ] Writing/typing/editing

[ ] Word processing

[ ] Data management/computer programming

[ ] Administrative/coordination

[ ] Reading

[ ] Research

[ ] Talking on the phone

[ ] Field visits

[ ] Thinking/planning

[ ] Other (please specify)

II. Please answer the following questions by selecting the answer which most closely fits your expectations.

| Strongly agree | Agree | Neutral | Disagree | Strongly disagree |
|---|---|---|---|---|

1. Adequate, clear communication between myself and my staff will be a problem when they telecommute.

| Strongly agree | Agree | Neutral | Disagree | Strongly disagree |
|---|---|---|---|---|
| [ ] | [ ] | [ ] | [ ] | [ ] |

2. I have a positive attitude towards telecommuting.

| [ ] | [ ] | [ ] | [ ] | [ ] |
|---|---|---|---|---|

3. Reduced professional interaction while telecommuting will be a problem for my staff.

| [ ] | [ ] | [ ] | [ ] | [ ] |
|---|---|---|---|---|

4. My staff will work well on their own while telecommuting.

| [ ] | [ ] | [ ] | [ ] | [ ] |
|---|---|---|---|---|

5. My staff will feel lonely when telecommuting.

   [ ]      [ ]      [ ]      [ ]      [ ]

6. If my staff telecommutes often, they will lose their identification with (or sense of belonging to) the county (company) system.

   [ ]      [ ]      [ ]      [ ]      [ ]

7. When my staff telecommutes, they will be less stressed.

   [ ]      [ ]      [ ]      [ ]      [ ]

III. Please answer the following questions by filling in the appropriate squares. There are no right or wrong answers.

8. Overall, my staff's productivity will ____ as a result of telecommuting.

   Increase [ ]     Stay the same [ ]     Decrease [ ]

9. The quality of my staff's work will ____ with telecommuting.

   Improve [ ]   Stay the same [ ]   Get worse [ ]

10. My staff will work _____ hours when telecommuting as compared to working in the office.

   More [ ]     The same [ ]     Less [ ]

11. My staff will complete _____ work when working at home than working at the office.

   More [ ]      The same [ ]      Less [ ]

12. My staff will be _____ motivated to work at home than at the office.

   More [ ]      Just as [ ]      Less [ ]

13. My staff with have _____ autonomy in carrying out assignments when telecommuting.

   More [ ]      The same [ ]      Less [ ]

14. My staff's morale will _____ as a result of telecommuting.

   Improve [ ]    Stay the same [ ]    Get worse [ ]

15. I will have _____ standards and expectations of my staff when they work at home compared to when they work in the office.

   Higher [ ]      The same [ ]      Lower [ ]

## *Telecommuting Survey for Employees*

We want to ask you about your attitudes and expectations telecommuting before participating in the project. You will be asked to complete a similar survey at the end of a one year period. All responses are confidential and will be used for statistical purposes only.

I.  General Information regarding your commute and telecommuting.

1.  How do you usually travel to work in a one week period? Please respond by indicating the percent of time you use each mode. If you always drive alone, your response will be 100% next to drive alone.

    _____ % Drive alone

    _____ % Car pool

    _____ % Van pool

    _____ % Public Bus

    _____ % Motorcycle

    _____ % Bicycle

    _____ % Walk

    _____ % Other (please specify)

2.  _____ How many miles do you travel to work?

    _____ How many miles one way?

3.  _____ How many minutes does it usually take you to get *to* work?

4.  _____ How many minutes does it usually take you to get home *from* work?

5.  _____ a.m. _____ p.m. What time do you usually arrive at work?

6.  _____ a.m. _____ p.m. What time do you usually leave work?

7. ____ yes ____ no   Have you telecommuted before?

8. ____ yes ____ no   Do you have a special room set aside for telecommuting at home?

9. ____ yes ____ no   Do you have a special area in a room set aside for telecommuting?

10. How do you feel about working for the county (company)?

[ ] very happy     [ ] happy     [ ] neutral
[ ] unhappy      [ ] very unhappy


II. Attitudinal Questions Regarding Telecommuting
    Part 1

Please answer the following questions by indicating whether you agree or disagree about the following statements. There are no right or wrong answers. Mark the category that most closely describes your *true* opinion.

1. Overall my job productivity will improve as a telecommuter.

| Strongly Agree | Agree | Neutral | Disagree | Strongly Disagree |
|:---:|:---:|:---:|:---:|:---:|
| [ ] | [ ] | [ ] | [ ] | [ ] |

2.  I will have problems getting my work completed on time as a telecommuter.

| Strongly Agree | Agree | Neutral | Disagree | Strongly Disagree |
|:---:|:---:|:---:|:---:|:---:|
| [ ] | [ ] | [ ] | [ ] | [ ] |

3.  Telecommuting will improve the quality of my work.

| Strongly Agree | Agree | Neutral | Disagree | Strongly Disagree |
|:---:|:---:|:---:|:---:|:---:|
| [ ] | [ ] | [ ] | [ ] | [ ] |

4.  I will not be likely to look for another job as long as I can telecommute.

| Strongly Agree | Agree | Neutral | Disagree | Strongly Disagree |
|:---:|:---:|:---:|:---:|:---:|
| [ ] | [ ] | [ ] | [ ] | [ ] |

5.  Some of my co-workers who cannot telecommute will be resentful of my telecommuting.

| Strongly Agree | Agree | Neutral | Disagree | Strongly Disagree |
|:---:|:---:|:---:|:---:|:---:|
| [ ] | [ ] | [ ] | [ ] | [ ] |

6.  Adequate, clear communication between me and my supervisor will be a problem when I telecommute.

| Strongly Agree | Agree | Neutral | Disagree | Strongly Disagree |
|:---:|:---:|:---:|:---:|:---:|
| [ ] | [ ] | [ ] | [ ] | [ ] |

7. My supervisor has a positive attitude towards telecommuting.

| Strongly Agree | Agree | Neutral | Disagree | Strongly Disagree |
|---|---|---|---|---|
| [ ] | [ ] | [ ] | [ ] | [ ] |

8. I will have a problem sharing office space when working in the office as a condition of telecommuting.

| Strongly Agree | Agree | Neutral | Disagree | Strongly Disagree |
|---|---|---|---|---|
| [ ] | [ ] | [ ] | [ ] | [ ] |

9. The lack of professional interaction while I telecommute will be a problem for me.

| Strongly Agree | Agree | Neutral | Disagree | Strongly Disagree |
|---|---|---|---|---|
| [ ] | [ ] | [ ] | [ ] | [ ] |

10. I will feel lonely when I telecommute.

| Strongly Agree | Agree | Neutral | Disagree | Strongly Disagree |
|---|---|---|---|---|
| [ ] | [ ] | [ ] | [ ] | [ ] |

11. If I telecommute often, I will lose my identification with, or sense of belonging to, the county (company).

| Strongly Agree | Agree | Neutral | Disagree | Strongly Disagree |
|---|---|---|---|---|
| [ ] | [ ] | [ ] | [ ] | [ ] |

12. The relationship between my supervisor and I will _____ as a result of telecommuting.

Improve [ ]     Stay the same [ ]     Get worse [ ]


III.  Background Information

This section collects background information on the telecommuters. This information will be used in comparing results of the telecommuting program to the general population. Please answer all questions, remember that your anonymity will be preserved in reporting responses. This data will only be used for statistical purposes. All this information is confidential.

1.  How old are you?
    [ ] Under 25          [ ] 40-44
    [ ] 25-29             [ ] 45-49
    [ ] 30-34             [ ] 50-54
    [ ] 35-39             [ ] 55-up

2.  Gender? [ ] male [ ] female

3.  What is your marital status?
    [ ] Single, never married
    [ ] Married
    [ ] Divorced
    [ ] Widowed
    [ ] Separated

4. Do you have children (under age 18) living at home?

   [  ] Yes                    [  ] No

   _____  How many children do you have living at home?

   _____  How many of them are five years old or younger?

5. Do you work full-time or part time?

   [  ] full-time    [  ] part time    [  ] other (specify)

6. _____ What is your home zip code?

7. How do you expect telecommuting to change your life style?

   _____

   _____

   _____

   _____

   _____

## The Results of the County of San Diego Telecommuting Pilot Project

By Spring of 1991, the County of San Diego determined that the telecommuting pilot project was an overwhelming success. The concept of telecommuting was fully accepted by the board of supervisors and is now being applied to all departments within the county's framework. At the time of this printing, complete statistics are not yet available as to the projected savings, nor have the percentages of traffic reduction been fully analyzed; but, predicated on the increase in employee production and the overall acceptance of the program by those who supervised as well as those who actually telecommuted, the county has concluded that all employees who qualify under the criteria established for telecommuting will be allowed the option of either working in the traditional office mode or, as the opportunity presents itself, to telecommute on a regular basis.

# Ambassador College and the SwifNet Project

Ambassador College is located in Pasadena, California. It is a relatively small institution and functions as the educational arm of the WorldWide Church of God. One of their responsibilities is the distribution of literature and magazines published by their church sponsor—literature which is advertised on their television program, "The World Tomorrow." This program, which deals primarily with current events as they relate to their church's views on Biblical prophecy, airs on as many as forty television stations at the same time. Because the literature offered is free and a toll-free number is offered to those viewers who wish to take advantage of this offer, the response to each offer is phenomenal. Each time the toll free number appeared on the screen, the college would receive approximately 250 calls per minute for a five to ten minute period of time. The

125 line telephone center in California was quickly swamped with callers each time a commercial aired.

To respond to this massive amount of calls, the college turned to its sister campus located in Big Sandy, Texas. The additional phone centre brought their total incoming lines up to 220. This number was still inadequate for the deluge of calls each commercial generated. Because the literature was free and the WorldWide Church of God is a nonprofit organization, it was difficult to justify the addition of new phone centres or new lines for the existing units. The college then conceived the inconceivable. It occurred to them that they could utilize the thousands of church supporters across America, supporters who would gladly volunteer their time and phone equipment, to aid the church in promoting its message.

Ambassador College envisioned a telecommunication network that would route incoming calls to the homes of the volunteer church members, allow the volunteers to answer the call on the first ring, take literature request information from the caller, and arrange to send the requested literature. It was also important to the College that supervisors be able to monitor the calls, listen in on new counselors to help in their training, and maintain the ability to intercede in a call when an emergency situation became evident. They needed a way for the volunteers to summon a supervisor and to alert that supervisor of the degree of urgency involved in the call. There had to be a way to differentiate between an information page and an emergency call.

Moreover, the college wanted the entire system to be completely transparent to the caller. The person responding to the offer for free literature must never know if the call is being answered by a bank of phone operators in Pasadena, a farmer's wife in Ohio, or a banker in Florida. In short, they needed speed and accuracy coupled with total transparency.

When Ambassador College went to AT&T and Pacific Bell, they were told that the technology did not exist that would allow them to do what they wanted done. After consulting with other telephone equipment and hardware suppliers, they came to realize that AT&T had been right. What they wanted just didn't exist. If they were determined to implement such a program, then they would have to design the system themselves.

Returning to their own laboratories on campus, a team of faculty scientists and students began working from the wish list the administration had given them. The result was a system that would eventually become known as SwifNet. Today, that system is being licensed and leased to many different telemarketing systems for dozens of different applications.

The significance of SwifNet is this. Now, for the first time, a telecommuter can stay inside his or her home and answer phones for a company literally across the nation or, for that matter, across the globe and have immediate access back to the mainframe and to central office assistance. They can be in constant touch with their supervisor and conduct business with nothing more than a touch-tone telephone which costs less than twenty dollars! The system requires virtually no technological knowledge beyond how to push a button on a telephone. SwifNet broke the last barrier—that need for high tech hard-

ware operated by low tech appliances located anywhere in the world. Within the next few years, as the
system is refined and as the next generation of software becomes available, the system will only get better. Telecommuters everywhere will benefit from this
technology.

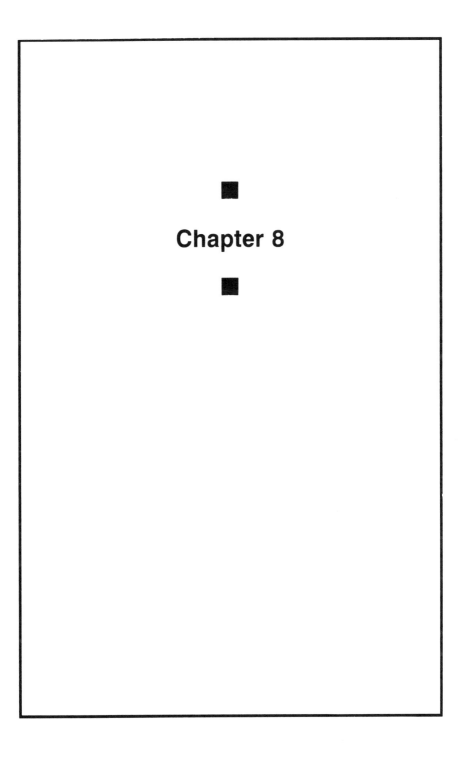

# Chapter 8

# A Study of Telecommuting as It Applies to Private Corporations

## Crane and Associates

Crane and Associates, a management company located in Menlo Park, California, specializes in consulting with other companies on how best they can comply with the laws of the State of California concerning trip reductions. Crane believes in telecommuting. While it is a relatively small company, it practices what it preaches. Two of their employees, one a mid-level executive and the other a senior transport planner, commute on a part-time basis.

The company first considered telecommuting to answer the direct threat of losing a valuable mid-level transportation planner. She lived in San Jose, about an hour and a half commute each way. Because of her high degree of specialization, handicapped transportation planning, it was imperative to Crane's continued participation in a large regional transportation planning development project that it not lose this employee. And it was in great danger of doing just that. By offering her the flexibility of telecommuting, Crane was able to keep a valued worker on the job—a worker who would have certainly sought employment elsewhere.

The other telecommuter is a retired senior transportation planner who lives in Berkeley, California—a drive which could easily take two hours each way. Since he works on a strictly part-time basis, on a project-by-project arrangement, it made good sense to keep this man by use of telecommuting. Without such a policy, both these employees would have relocated to jobs nearer their homes.

Undeniably, Crane and Associates turned to telecommuting because of employee retention. This *was* the motivating factor, but not the only factor. In both cases, productivity increased, while stress and fear of burn-out was greatly decreased. Crane now has a company policy concerning telecommuting which encourages its employees to telecommute on a part-time basis.

Crane has a vested interest in seeing the telecommuting concept accepted throughout its region. It is one of the solutions it offers other companies when they are consulted for suggestions in trip and traffic reductions. This company is a prime example of the first rule of telecommuting. For telecommuting to be effective, it must mutually benefit all parties concerned.

# California Western Life— Worst Case Scenario

California Western Life was a claims processing firm headquartered in Sacramento, California. Their largest single client was the State of California. They had bid for and received a contract to process all the health claims for state employees—a contract which was, in and of itself, lucrative enough to insure the company's continued growth. California Western became a beehive of activity, and a model of growth. But it didn't stop there! It was destined to become another model, a model of what can happen when telecommuting goes awry.

Cal-West began its telecommuting program in 1982. Twenty-five employees were given the choice of leaving their traditional jobs and opting for the privilege of working at home. The difference in Cal-West's approach and that of other successful telecommuting firms is that Cal-West saw telecommuting primarily as a means to cut business expenses, while not giving equal consideration to the long-term well-being of its employees. Cal-West took the position that those telecommuters were no longer part of the corporate structure, but rather independent contractors. As such, Cal-West reasoned, those workers were no longer eligible to be compensated as employees; that is, they no longer would receive the fringe benefits that often comprise a large portion of the total compensation package. No more paid vacations, no more paid holidays, no free group insurance, no sick days; in short, they were on their own.

It was Cal-West's contention that those workers would now be able to make substantially more money for both the company and themselves now that they were freed from the constrictions of an office environment. The workers were told they could work as much and as long as they wished. There was a minimum level of work, however, which must be maintained in order to retain their work-at-home status; but, that minimum was set only to insure that the company's investment in time and equipment was not wasted. Beyond the minimum, there was no limit as to the amount of work the telecommuter could turn in. Theoretically, if an independent contractor wanted to work twenty-four hours a day, seven days a week, it was fine with Cal-West. They were, after all, paying for the work done, not the hours spent. And there was a great deal of work to do. The company leased a computer terminal to the home workers which was connected to the main frame in Cal-West's central offices. It seemed like a deal made in heaven. At the outset, everyone was happy. There appeared to be no losers in this arrangement. But soon, within two years of the start-up of the plan, trouble was brewing.

At this point, California Western's story takes two forks depending on whether one's sympathies lay with the workers or the company. Eight of the telecommuters filed suit in California State Court. The suit, *Paula Edwards, et. al.,* vs *California Western States Life,* alleged the company deliberately mislead the workers when they encouraged them to become telecommuters. The plaintiffs further alleged that the defendant did not inform them of the benefits they were giving up, selling them the "sizzle" but not the "steak." The defendant, however, pointed out that each employee was given full disclosure of what rights they were forfeiting and what benefits they were gaining; moreover, each worker had signed a contract to that effect.

It was the plaintiff's contention that these workers were not represented by counsel when they signed their contracts and, therefore out of ignorance, were cheated and robbed of their inalienable rights as workers. The defendant countered by pointing out the obvious: these workers were not children, but rather mature, thinking individuals with every opportunity to consider and weigh the options for each style of work. Further, they took solace in the fact that even while these defendants were engaged in litigation, there was a waiting list of employees wanting to begin the telecommuting program themselves. Of the original twenty-five who had begun this program, only eight were parties to the lawsuit. The other seventeen had either retired or were still in the program.

The defendant claimed the suit was based only on a few workers' attempts to squeeze money out of the corporate treasury. The plaintiffs' claim was based on the company's lack of compassion and apparent cavalier attitude toward the concept of fair play. The original suit was for a total of $1.25 million. The case settled out of court, with the details of the settlement placed under a "gag" order. While the exact amount of money California Western paid out will never be known publicly, it is conceded by both parties to be "less than what was sought, but more than was initially offered."

Perhaps the most interesting outcome of this case was that it had no negative impact on the telecommuting industry other than to point out to potential employers the dangers and pitfalls which must be avoided when such programs are initiated and implemented. Ultimately, Cal-West stopped doing business in the State of California, but it is doubtful that this was a result of the law-suit.

A great deal about the nature and the essence of telecommuting and telecommuters can be learned from this case. It was, without a doubt, the "worst-case" scenario which can arise out of a telecommuting program. But it need not have been. Had California Western been more selective in their choice of workers, had they defined more precisely at the outset what they expected and were prepared to accept in the areas of work completion, error acceptance, and payment schedules much of the misunderstanding which ultimately led to a courtroom battle could have been avoided.

*The burden for the successful implementation of any telecommuting program falls squarely on the shoulders of the company, never on the backs of the workers!* This is not to say there is no responsibility on the part of the workers to help make sure the program succeeds; but it is not fair, nor does it make sound business sense to expect the worker to carry the brunt of the decision-making process and to be held responsible for corporate decisions. The company, and only the company, can dictate policy and regulations. These rules should be spelled out in plain language, as simply as possible, but as thoroughly as necessary to prevent what happened to California Western from happening to other companies.

# The Travelers Group— A Study in Perfection

If California Western is an example of a telecommuters worst nightmare, it can be balanced by a study of The Travelers Group, based in Hartford, Connecticut. The Travelers has been a textbook case of efficiency, fairness, and application of technology in relation to human resources. Since it began its telecommuting program in 1986, each succeeding year has seen an increase in the number of participants and a marked increase in productivity for all departments involved.

The Travelers has two levels of telecommuters. A part-time telecommuter is one who works less than four days a week away from the office. A full-time home worker comes into the office only one-half day per week. It is not unusual for company officers to telecommute, although usually on a part-time basis. The Travelers has two types of full-time telecommuters. The traditional home-worker, one who lives within commuting range of the main office, and the long distance worker, who may live as far away as Florida or California. The success of their program lies primarily in the company's ability to be flexible in its relations regarding policy for telecommuting employees. While telecommuting within this company is limited to only two departments, by the turn of the century, management envisions that many more divisions will be involved in this program.

The Travelers rarely *hires* a telecommuter. Most of its telecommuters have been with the company at least a year before they are considered for telecommuting. It prefers to "grow" its own home workers based on the individual employee's needs and desires. This is an integral key to the success telecommuting has enjoyed in this company. By taking only trained employees, those who have a proven work history, and carefully grooming those workers for telecommuting, the company stands a much better chance of the worker being successful once he or she is introduced to the home environment. The company provides a great deal of education and counseling for the departing office worker and, in doing such, prepares the worker for what he or she might expect once the employee is on his or her own. Both the worker and his or her supervisor are given the opportunity to discuss what the expectations of the telecommuting job will be, as well as how each intends to fulfill those expectations.

Shortly after the implementation of The Travelers program, the company did two surveys which included both employees and managers. These studies yielded very positive feedback concerning telecommuting. The primary difference between The Travelers and other companies which have turned to telecommuting is that The Travelers consider the primary function of any telecommuting program to be employee retention. With the use of flexible work hours and work locations, the company is able to attract and to keep a better grade of workers. They regard the other obvious benefits— increased productivity and decreased costs—to be secondary to the company's need for continuity in its more specialized work areas, particularly that of computer programing and design.

The Travelers have made a concerted effort to be cognizant of the fact that often an employee who telecommutes is penalized by lack of promotion. They realize that high visibility is often a key factor in who is promoted and, as importantly, who is not. To this end, workers who engage in telecommuting are evaluated in the same way and with the same measurement as are the more traditional workers. Aiding in this effort to remain fair toward all employees is the fact that The Travelers already has two career paths in place for its employees. The first, called the "technical" path, is for employees whose jobs deal with the more creative aspect of the company, such as computer programmers and systems analysts. The second, or the "traditional" path, consists of those employees whose jobs are more rigorously defined, workers such as claims processors or data entry personnel.

By dividing their employees into these two groups, the company has replaced the normal bias which would exist in most corporate arenas against telecommuters in regard to promotions. They have also managed to build into the employer-employee relationship a concept of fair play, and this has resulted in a heightened degree of employee loyalty which manifests itself in a lower incidence of employee turnover. This added bonus contributes significantly to an increase in productivity which is a direct result of less on-the-job training and the use of more experienced personnel, particularly in highly specialized areas of employment.

# Megatek Industries

Perhaps the strangest motivation for setting up a telecommuting program came from Megatek Industries, San Diego, California. In 1981, long before telecommuting was a national buzzword, Megatek at that time faced what seemed three insurmountable problems. One of their managers, a man deeply involved in a highly sensitive research and development program, was the victim of a foiled murder attempt. The perpetrator, an ex-employee of Megatek, was released on bail, and the manager, rather than face another possible attempt on his life, decided he would leave San Diego. Such a move would ordinarily have precluded his continued employment with Megatek. Megatek was not willing, however, to lose such a valued employee. After a meeting of top management, the director of human resources for Megatek suggested that perhaps the employee in question could be relocated in another city and continue his work via computer lines.

It was a radical solution to a radical problem. If Megatek needed more prodding, that prodding came in the form of a second emergency situation which came on the heels of the first problem. Megatek received a contract to design a software package for another company. The software was to be completed in a specified period of time in order that it would coincide with another project that company was developing. To miss that deadline would have resulted

in a terrific financial liability to Megatek. Very often
in the rapidly evolving world of technological advances, software that is not developed in a timely
fashion runs the risk of becoming obsolete before it
is off the drawing board. Three of the five designers
working on this particular project became pregnant
at the same time. All three would need to take ma-
ternity leave and when they left, even if they could
have been replaced, the project would be set back at
least a year. Once more, Megatek looked at
telecommuting and found their answer. All three
women agreed to continue the project via modems
and personal computers from their homes. It was at
this point Megatek moved wholeheartedly into
telecommuting, breaking new ground in a trend
which, in the coming decade, would become a mainstay of modern business!

Megatek became an early study in the problems
which are part and parcel of telecommuting, and it
found the solutions for these problems quickly. The
first wrinkle in the plan was that no one foresaw
how isolated the home workers would soon become.
Megatek solved this problem by hosting weekly
lunches during which both the office staff and the
telecommuting staff would come together, face to
face, and discuss the problems with the project, as
well as catch up on office gossip, scandals, and politics, which, like it or not, are a reality in corporate
life. The weekly luncheon became a release valve for
the home workers, providing them with the much
needed social contact as well as maintaining a line of
communication with the office bound worker that
has since proven an integral part of any telecommuting project.

In the beginning, telecommuting was a gender bi-
ased program. It seemed to have greater appeal to
women, particularly those women who were mothers
of small children. California Western Life knew this,
as did many companies whose primary purpose for
moving into the world of telecommuting centered on
employee retention. To this end, most companies
promoted telecommuting as an alternative to child
care and, in many cases, as a viable option to mater-
nity leave or early retirement. It is a well established
fact that the bulk of employee related expenses from
the employer's standpoint comes directly from training and retraining workers to do the same job. No
employer wants to lose a trained employee, especially when that training is in the form of technological practices peculiar to that employer. When
companies first moved toward telecommuting, their
first conception of where this alternative mode of
employment could best be deployed invariably centered around the young married woman, the employee most likely to become pregnant, hence, most
likely to leave the company after receiving the training and specialization germane to that company.

Soon though, it became apparent that gender was
not the primary determination in the selection of
personnel for telecommuting. Other factors came
into play, the final considerations were: increased
production and employee retention. Today, these are
still the principle reasons any company turns to
home working as an alternate work style. Under-
standably, those companies which have enjoyed the
greatest degree of success in telecommuting are the
very ones which choose not to make public their
commitment to the program. This is based on the

fact that often telecommuting is the competitive edge which makes companies using it more productive and more efficient than their competitors. For this reason, many companies, such as Scientific Applications Inc. (S.A.I.), often will not discuss their program or will conceal its use by means of alternate descriptions of their company's policies. S.A.I. prefers to consider each of their telecommuters as "branch office" managers thus allowing its use of telecommuters to be a hidden asset while, at the same time, giving the appearance of being a much larger company than it really is. It may list in its public relations releases that it has offices in several states and dozens of locations. In reality, these "branch" offices are nothing more than the location of one or more telecommuters. By strict definition, each home worker is, in essence, a remote location from which the company does indeed conduct business.

Soon, Megatek had other employees applying for home worker status. They crossed the gender barrier when a young male employee, a software writer, wanted to return to Stanford University in order to continue his education. Instead of losing this bright worker, Megatek hooked up a personal computer and a modem which allowed this employee to link his apartment at Stanford with Megatek's office in San Diego. The results were spectacular! Megatek managed to keep a valuable worker, the employee was able to further his education, and production was enhanced by the arrangement. Everyone involved was pleased with the results of the move.

Megatek felt there were four important factors which made telecommuting a viable concept. It fostered a sense of teamwork, allowed group continuity, promoted the best gathering of talent possible, and most important, it made employee retention an attainable goal.

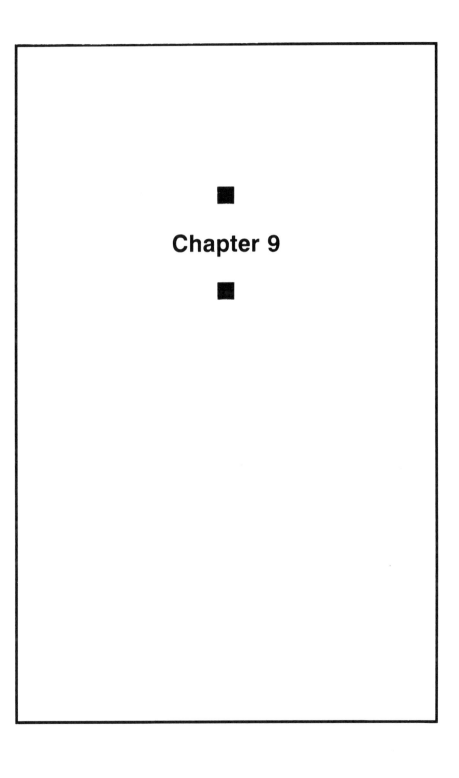

# Chapter 9

# Telecommuting as a Means of Legislative Compliance

The Americans with Disabilities Act of 1991 contained some very dramatic and radical concepts, not the least of which addressed the issue of employers' obligations to what is commonly referred to as the "handicapped." In essence, any employer with over fifteen employees fell under this new umbrella—an umbrella designed to prohibit discrimination against the 2.8 million workers who are classified by this designation. Particularly abrasive to most employers is the fact that when any handicapped person who is denied employment for any reason brings a discrimination suit against the company who denied them a job, it then becomes the company's burden to prove the handicapped individual was denied a job because of other considerations, not because of their impairment. In short, the burden of proof now falls on the accused, not the accuser!

Telecommuting may well be the ultimate answer to this dilemma. While architectual barriers are often difficult to remove and facilities to aid the handicapped are often nearly impossible to install within the existing framework of a corporate office building, phone lines run everywhere! It may well be that the time has come which will allow American business to extend to all people the opportunity to earn a living regardless of their physical disabilities. Telecommuting can be done by virtually anyone; if a physical handicap is all that separates a worker from his job, that barrier will come crashing to the ground with the advent of telecommuting.

## Federal Statutes Concerning Telecommuting

There is very little legislation now enacted concerning the issue of telecommuting. As time passes and as more corporations embrace the practice of using home workers, it is reasonable to expect this situation will change. Very little congressional investigation has been conducted on this topic. A notable exception to this was a study by the Committee on Government Operations, in July of 1986. The subcommittee on Employment and Housing issued a report entitled, "Home-Based Workers: Are They Victims of Exploitation?" The report noted that young women with young children comprised the fastest growing segment of the workforce, and that, as such, alternative modes of employment for these people would soon become of major concern to both the private as well as the public sector of labor employing entities.

The tone of the report was negative. It pointed to some rather atypical scenarios of workers who were indeed exploited by the companies for whom they worked. It went into great detail outlining the means and procedures by which these workers were victimized by those various and sundry companies. Testimony was taken from a woman who had worked as an in-home typist transcribing documents for a large company. The woman testified that she had rented a typewriter from her employer at a cost of $845.00 a year. She found that under the "work-at-home" arrangement she had signed with her former employer, she now worked more hours, often late into the night, and on weekends, only to keep up with the work load the company expected her to produce. She claimed to be under a great deal of stress and likened her position to her employer as analogous to a coal miner's relationship with the company store.

Testimony was also taken from a telecommunications expert who listed several advantages to telecommuting, among them the ability for mothers with small children to find employment as well as people previously considered unemployable because of economic, social, and physical disadvantages. This expert also testified that there were a great number of advantages to employers using this alternate employment style—advantages which did not result in the usual offsetting disadvantages to the workers. He cited increased productivity, less economic outlay to go to work, less pollution, less congestion, and, lastly, the company's ability to retain employees who might have otherwise left the corporation without the flexibility telecommuting offers.

The report closed with the onerous warning that at some time in the near future legislation would probably need be passed in order to protect the rights of the workers.

## The United States Tax Code as an Instrument of Change

One of the congressmen who worked on the above mentioned sub-committee was Representative Beau Boulter of Texas. He, along with four other representatives, wrote the minority report that accompanied the House report concerning home workers. Mr. Boulter has said that if the future of business lies along the path of the electronic cottage, then the tax code is the place that the changes will take place. It would be a simple matter for the tax code to allow employers significant tax credits and deductions for the establishment of home-based workers, especially if these workers are in some way considered disadvantaged.

Moreover, the minority report, while admitting that the potential for abuse was present in any system that allowed the company to determine who is and who isn't an employee, determined the overall effect of this trend would be to employ more people, reduce pollution, and help make American businesses more competitive on the world market. The report also pointed to the fact that the United States government is experimenting with various forms of this concept and that in time, certainly by the end of the twentieth century, telecommuting will no longer be considered an oddity, but rather, a normal way of doing business.

## Support from the President of the United States

George Bush, in the spring of 1990, spoke to a bipartisan group of business men at the California Chamber of Commerce on the subject of telecommuting. Bush said, "Consider this: A typical twenty minute round-trip to work over the course of a year adds up to two very stressful 40-hour weeks lost on the road. If only 5 percent of the commuters in L.A. County telecommuted one day each week, they'd save 205 million miles of travel each year, and keep 47,000 tons of pollutants from entering the atmosphere. Telecommuting means saving energy, improving air quality, and quality of life. Not a bad deal."

This statement of support will in all likelihood result in legislative action. There are ramifications to the President's statement which will reach beyond the mere endorsement of a new idea; they will manifest themselves in things such as building materials and building codes which, in some cities, already call for the installation of fiber optic wiring in all new construction of residential and commercial property.

Moreover, legislative action is already pending in six
states concerning tax breaks for telecommuters
based on the number of miles saved each year.
Three states have legislative committees studying
the feasibility of anti-credit discrimination laws for
businesses which operate from their homes, and
nineteen states have on-going investigations concerning the growing health insurance crisis and how
it impacts those who work at home.

## Organized Labor and Its Position
## in Regard to Telecommuting

As might be expected, at first organized labor was
not enthralled with the idea of telecommuting. Obviously, once the worker moves out of the office and
into his home, he is less likely to see a need for
union representation. Moreover, labor leaders tend
to see the advent of the home office site as an ugly
reincarnation of the sweat shops which existed in
this country until the fourth decade of this century.
It was to ban unfair labor practices that the Fair
Labor Standards Act of 1938 (FLSA) was passed.
This legislation in effect outlawed the manufacturing
of seven distinct items of clothing outside the confines of a commercial factory or assembly area. This
legislation was necessitated by the fact that some
garment manufacturers used home workers as a
means to avoid the minimum hourly wage, payroll
taxes, and social security benefit contributions.

In 1938, such concern for the workers was justified. America was yet to recover from the staggering
effects of the depression, and World War II was still

three years away. High immigration figures made for a very competitive marketplace, where one ethnic group vied against another for the opportunity to work in a factory for twenty-five cents an hour. Only blue collar workers were protected under the FLSA, and it refered only to those engaged in the manufacture of such items as knitted outerwear, women's outerware, jewelry making, gloves and mittens, buttons and buckles fabrications, handkerchief sewing and embroidery. Those workers who had previously worked in these industries were forced to go back to the factories to perform their jobs.

This return to structured hours and production reduced the opportunity for employers to exploit workers. Today, however, the situation is radically different. Today, the average telecommuter is not blue collar, but rather white collar or what is now used in the vernacular of the industry, "open collar." He or she is likely to be well educated, if not a holder of one or more degrees. Today's home worker chooses to work at home for social or other reasons which most often have nothing to do with economics. Today's companies will often provide extra benefits to secure a worker willing to perform his job from his home. In short, there are virtually no similarities between the exploited home worker of the thirties and the modern telecommuter of the nineties.

These facts did nothing to deter the unions from making one last-ditch effort to run telecommuting aground. On October 6, 1983, the 15th Constitutional Convention of the AFL-CIO meeting in Hollywood, Florida, passed what was titled an "AFL-CIO Resolution on Computer Home Work." The resolution, in essence, called for an extension of the ban on home working outlined in the Fair Labor Standards Act of 1938 to include home workers whose job is performed by or on computers. Citing the fact that by the year 1990 (at that time, still seven years away), the Bureau of Labor Statistics predicted computer occupations will have been increasing nearly three times as fast as the expected rate of growth for all occupations in the economy. The AFL-CIO felt there was no doubt, given the history of home working, that these people would become open game for exploitation by their employers:

> The piecework nature of computer work increases the risk of employee exploitation. The worker is under constant surveillance by supervisors through the terminal, and it is a short step from evaluating workers by output to paying them by output.

In that same paragraph, the resolution went on to lay the foundation of the union's real objections:

"They will be isolated in their homes, making union organizing and other concerted activity difficult."

The resolution ended with this admonition:

"Resolved, the AFL-CIO calls for an early ban on computer home work by the Department of Labor as a measure of protection for those workers entering the market for the fastest-growing occupation in the United States."

Six years later, the 18th Constitutional Convention of the AFL-CIO was convened. Among the business undertaken by that convention was to restate the union's changing position *vis-a-vis* the question of home workers. In the six years that had elapsed, the union's position concerning home working had weakened to the point that it realized it could not hope to bind together these home workers into a single union, nor would its unions be strong enough to push congress into a ban on what was shaping up to be a condition of employment for people who were essentially not the typical labor union member. They adopted a different tact, opting for legislative control rather than legislative ban on the industry:

> We urge the establishment of appropriate new regulations on home work to prevent exploitation of workers in offices as well as factories. Special provisions should be provided for the handicapped.

This new approach represented a realistic view of the situation. It called upon the Federal government to serve as the watchdog over the activities of the home workers rather than the labor unions. Moreover, it put employers on notice that while the unions were, for the moment giving up on trying to ban home computer workers, they were not giving up on legislative recourses.

According to the Office of the Director of Public Policy for the Service Employees Union in Washington, D.C., the unions have come to understand both the need for telecommuters and the reality of their numbers. The only regulations that the SEU considers to be of any real significance are those concerning wage and hours. It feels that the level of sophistication of the modern office worker tend to

make him or her less susceptible to victimization by
the companies for whom he or she works. Any effective legislation will be in the area of ensuring that
off-site workers maintain a parity with those workers
left in the office. Anything less than parity will result, in the union's opinion, in the creation of a
second-rate employee class.

Labor unions are paper tigers in this particular
arena. A spokesperson for the International Ladies
Garment Workers Union stated:

> No one in the labor movement wants to ex-
> tend the ban on home workers to the
> telecommuter industry. No union is going to
> waste its time or money trying to get legisla-
> tion passed which has no chance of passage.

Essentially, this is the prevailing attitude which all
unions are adopting today. This is not to say that at
a later date the unions won't once more try to make
an end-run at the telecommuter industry. By virtue
of their numbers, telecommuters would make a
plum in any union's basket. But the facts are plain.
Most telecommuters are not union material. This is
based both on the type of workers involved as well as
the nature of their work.

If your company has a union contract now, it is
likely that the union will make an attempt to impose
some sanctions on your telecommuting efforts; but,
these sanctions will be baseless without the support
of the union's leaders and, as of now, the leaders are
not inclined to tilt at windmills. If unions are a major
player in your office, consider taking them into your
confidence as you plan your telecommuter program.

Point out the fact that the employee will likely bene-fit as much if not more than the company from such a program. Remember, the simple truth is that telecommuting is outside the grasp of the union's reach!

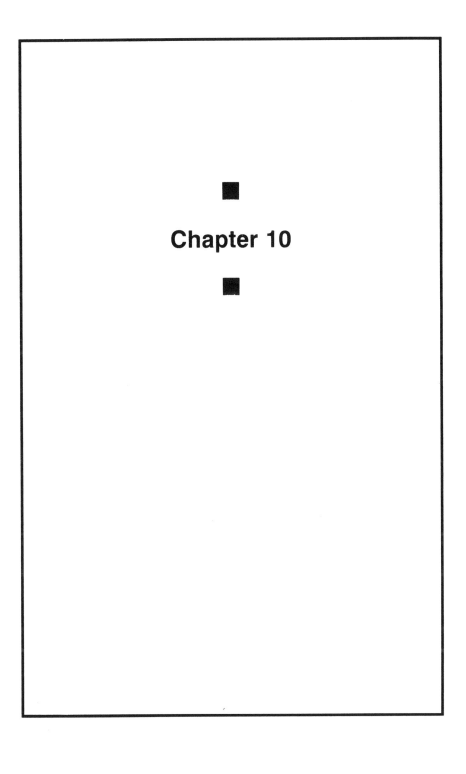

# Chapter 10

# The Global Implications of Telecommuting as It Relates to the 21st Century

## Telecommuting as It Relates to a Global Economy

One of the more unusual aspects of telecommuting is that it transcends national borders. It respects neither distance nor cultures. Inasmuch as Americans are no longer a society of producers—that is, a people whose primary function is to manufacture tangible hard-goods, products such as automobiles, airplanes, brooms, dishwashers, or paper—we find ourselves in a position of transition. We are becoming a nation whose emphasis is shifting from the manufacturing of products to the application and service of those products manufactured by others. Our involvement in these products enhances their ultimate value. In essence, we are rapidly becoming a nation of information processors. We process raw data in much the same manner as we once processed raw cotton. It is a fact of life in the United States that more people can operate office machinery than run a tractor, drive a commercial truck, or assemble a finished product for the use of a consumer across the nation or across the world.

We've become a vast repository of information and data, and that information must be melded into a useable form each and every day of the year. As computers become the ultimate rulers of our lives (and if you think they're not, try to explain to a utility company that your bill is incorrect, or tell a bank that there is an error in your checking account), it is clearly of critical importance that data is fed into the machines as quickly as it is gathered. In some cases, the data collection and entry are done in the same step, such as a charge on a credit card made through the use of a touch tone telephone. When the buyer enters the product code for the item via telephone or modem, he or she follows that entry with a credit card number and any other pertinent information required by the host system. When the charge is completed, it is inputed into a central commuter and billed to the purchaser's account. The amount of the charge is deducted from the purchaser's credit line while simultaneously being credited to the seller's account. A new credit line is established, based on the amount of unused credit available on the account—all without a human being ever seeing the transaction, all with the speed of sound!

Beyond the obvious fact that information movement is the next revolution in store for American business, is that America is quickly moving into the sphere of service oriented commerce. As we become a nations of consumers rather than producers, service industries become focal points for evolutionary and revolutionary change. Service industries are quite different from other cash generating endeavors, such as manufacturing, agricultural enterprises, and food processing, in as much as service oriented corporations produce economic advantages without producing any tangible products. Some of these services, such as retail sales, transportation, and food preparation, enhance the basic value of a manufactured product by placing the aforementioned product in the hands of the consumer in such a manner that the product is now ready for consumption either as a durable good or in the form of a readily useable product, such as a dinner.

While some services enhance a manufactured product's usability, other service oriented industries have virtually little or nothing to do with a finished product. Insurance, finance, and wholesale distribution operations are examples of these. Those services which are dependent on the enhancement of a manufactured good tend to be limited regarding the scope of the distance where the goods are utilized as opposed to service companies which provide less visible support and, therefore, can be performed from distances far greater than the heretofore mentioned.

# Five Factors Most Responsible for the Increased Competition in the World Economy

The direct relationship which exists between finished goods and services will be the final determining factor in whether or not that service is one which will need protection from foreign firms offering that service. As the concept of global competition grows, there are five factors which repeatedly surface determining the feasibility of that service as a global commodity—that is whether or not that service is "telecommutable." The first of these five is the integrated world market. Before a service can be considered to be international in scope, it must first have an application in more than one country and have markets in a multitude of economic stratum existing within the confines of those other nations. Telephone service is an excellent example of global integration. There is not a nation on earth that does not in one fashion or another connect itself with the rest of the world through telecommunications. And telephone service is one which cuts through most economic barriers within those countries to the point that in most nations telephone service is taken for granted; it is almost as common as electricity and running water.

The second factor which has resulted in increased competition among world economies is the oversupply of goods and manufactured products. As more nations join the family of industrialized countries, each new addition tends to develop the same basic industries. In most commodities, this is of little consequence. In some areas, however, the newness of the manufacturing installations coupled with an advancement of technological upgrading tends to boost the productivity of the new plant thereby giving the newest entry into a particular field a temporary advantage—an advantage which often leads to overproduction and, consequently, a decrease in the price of that item. Again, this factor is a temporary one, and as prices decline, production quotas deteriorate allowing for a downturn in inventory levels which results in price stabilization.

The third factor, and perhaps one of the more prevalent trends in Western nations, is the decline of the power previously exercised by labor unions. As emerging third world nations begin to crowd into the market place offering cheaper goods predicated on the utilization of cheap labor, those with like goods produced in countries whose factories are burdened with the excess fat which labor unions force upon management during contract negotiations are squeezed out of the market place. This ultimately results in the closing of those factories and eventually leads to the demise of those very unions whose insistence upon unreasonable demands brought on their own destruction.

The fourth factor leading to tighter competition in the global marketplace deals with a growing increase in most Western nations to deregulate various industries in favor of an attitude more consistent with laissez-faire economic controls. In the United States, the airline industry is a prime example of what deregulation of one industry can ultimately do to a world market. By allowing the airlines to seek their own level of competence, set their own prices, routes, and schedules in global travel as well as national operations, the airlines of America have been instrumental in an overall deregulation of most airlines throughout the free world. An airline based in Germany cannot charge more for service between Frankfort and New York then an American company does. If they do, they won't book the passage; the American company will. This type of pressure is a perfect example of deregulation in one country causing a ripple effect to flow through other countries as well.

The fifth factor which caused a sudden escalation of global price wars is the privatization of government and industry. It is a given that the private sector of any industry will outperform that same industry when placed under the control of any central government. Compare the delivery of documents and parcels when handled between two governments as opposed to that same parcel being delivered by Federal Express or The Flying Tigers. It becomes painfully obvious; there is no comparison. One is a model of efficiency and a prototype of capitalism at work. The other is an exercise in wasted motions and governmental duplication, inefficiency, and waste.

As these five factors work hand-in-hand, the end result is a marked increase in the competition between companies located in different countries. In the absence of some form of protective tariffs or restrictive competitive laws, each country's fortunes will rise or fall in direct relation to its ability to muster a higher degree of productivity within their industries than their competing countries. Because of this, it is imperative that the United States not sit quietly by and wait as the competition walks away with the gold while it weighs the risks and benefits of restrictive tariffs and non-competing laws in regard to our own industries at home. Telecommuting will give America the competitive edge it needs to effectively compete in the global marketplace.

# Service Industries in the United States by the Year 1993

Consider this. According to the U.S. Bureau of Labor Statistics, the nine largest service industries are:

| Industry | Millions of Employees |
|---|---|
| Retail Trade | 12.5 |
| Education | 9.1 |
| Health Care | 8.0 |
| General Government | 7.7 |
| Finance, Insurance, Real Estate | 6.4 |
| Restaurants and Bars | 6.0 |
| Wholesale Trade | 5.9 |
| Transportation and Public Utilities | 5.8 |
| Business Services | 5.0 |

Virtually every one of these industries will in some way lend themselves to telecommuting. Each of these business categories employs workers in the field of sales, planning, advertising, promotions, designs, and computer data processing. *And each of these fields are easily adapted to telecommuting.* Add the total people involved in these industries and the figure will exceed 65 million workers. If only 25 percent of these applied telecommuting techniques to their jobs, it would mean an additional 16 million home workers.

A goodly number of these jobs need not be done anywhere near where the services are actually offered. The insurance and financial workers need not be on-site, nor even in the same state where the institutions for whom they work maintain corporate offices. The same can be said for a large percentage of business services, education services, health care support services, and public utilities. The obvious danger here is that while this work can be inputed from across town, across state, or across country, it can also be inputed from across the globe!

If it is a given that industry and commerce places their greatest concern on bottom-line profits, then it is also a given that they will seek to increase these profits by cutting their labor expenses whenever possible. Now comes the rub! Keyboard operators in mainland China are compensated at a rate of $5.00 U.S. per day, for a ten-hour day. Jamaican workers are paid $10.00 U.S. per day for a ten-hour day. Now what will compel an American based, multinational company to hire U.S. workers at a rate ten times as high and for only 80 percent of the work day as they could a foreign worker? Frankly, it is a difficult situation, one which will require cooperation of not only the companies involved, but the workers of that company, the United States Government, and the labor unions of America.

Protectionism tends to be seen as a dirty word. As Americans, we seem to have the concept that open competition is almost always the clearest and cheapest avenue to pursue. Other nations, however, view the question of telecommuting as well as international cross-employment in an entirely different light. Canada's Parliment passed a law in 1980 (The 1980 Bank and Bank Revision Act) which prohibits the use of foreign data entry which in any way impacts banks, financial lending institutions, and insurance companies. Moreover, it compels the use of Canadian labor in all transactions which concern governmental documentation. In effect, the Canadians have chosen to keep Canadian telecommuting a family affair, restricting the amount of international influence in their financial and legal documentation.

Canada is not alone in this rationale. Many nations, among them Brazil, Argentina, and dozens of third world nations, have laws prohibiting any foreign companies from providing technical services unless there are no national firms able to do so. This practice serves two purposes. First, it wrests control over integral portions of a nation's economy out of the hands of foreigners, where it really has no business being in the first place; and secondly, it encourages the local business community to "grow" its own people—people who will clearly have the ability and expertise to carry forth the objectives of their company and, ultimately, their nation's economic growth.

If countries as diverse in their social and economic development as Canada, France, and Zimbabwe all see the wisdom in effecting such protectionism, why can't we, in the U.S., see the same thing? For too long we have railed against the idea of closing our markets to other nations. We have resisted the idea of making it more difficult for foreign concerns to compete with American businesses. Perhaps this is the time, perhaps telecommuting is the cause. We cannot depend on foreign governments to place the needs of our country ahead of the economic growth of theirs. Our only path through this junction will be with legislation and with the sincerest efforts of labor, management, and government. Any other approach will fall miserably short. If we fail to act now, while this new industry is still an infant, it is certain that what will evolve will be a repetition of the sweat shops of the early twentieth century where the threat of cheaper and cheaper labor ultimately pits one people against another. The end product will be a situation where no one makes a decent living and society, in general, suffers.

From this standpoint, telecommuting does pose a threat to the continued economic growth of the inner cities as well as a potential danger to the economic safety of the corporations who choose to use this type of labor pool. Because of refinements and advancements in the use of satellite communications, fiber optic transmission lines, and the availability of telecommuting devices found even in the most remote of global locations, no financial enterprise will ever again be limited in scope solely because of geographic settings. The advent of the new Common Market, a feat as much in communications as it is in economics, will further harness the powers of telecommuting. One common European currency, one common European form of business management, and one common European economic goal, will make for a skillful competitor and a powerful ally.

# Telecommuting Experiments in Europe

Telecommuting in Europe is becoming a rather commonplace event. The same driving forces behind the movement in the United States exist in Europe. Gasoline is three to five times more expensive on the continent than it is in the U.S. Traffic congestion, smog, and an increasingly competitive economy are all factors which spell out the need for telecommuting in Europe. In addition, other problems exist which are unique to that part of the world. Automobile fumes, for example, are considered the major environmental threat to the art and sculpture of the old world. European art and artifacts, relics of eras gone by, are at risk from an air supply heavily laden with fluorocarbons. There is no way to avoid the impending crisis with air pollution and excessive fuel prices unless trip reductions efforts are taken seriously.

## The Netherlands

A study was recently conducted by the Ministry of Transport for the Netherlands. The RIV, a department which oversees transportation and is charged with the task of finding ways to increase trip reduction, has reached many of the same conclusions which American governmental bodies have come to realize as truth. There is a definite correlation between telecommuting and increased productivity. Thirty-one employees of the RIV telecommuted for a

period of nine months. Trip reductions by the participants of the survey revealed a total mileage reduction of over 25 percent, and these miles were saved
by commuters during rush hour, which in comparison to our rush hour makes our freeways seem like
the Indy 500. One main difference between the approach Europeans are taking as compared to their
American counterparts is that in Europe, the idea of
the satellite office, or the "work-o-tels," has gained
greater popularity.

The same concerns and fears exist in Europe as do
in the Uniter' States. Quoting from a report by the
Ministry of Transport in The Netherlands:

> Telecommuting is not a new kind of house
> industry, in the traditional meaning of that
> word. There one refers to relatively simple
> tasks, (shrimp peeling, sewing) done by
> piece-workers who are not part of an organi-
> zation. Of old this kind of work is in bad
> standing. The Ministry of Social Affairs and
> the unions wish to prevent that the same
> happens to telecommuting.

The report goes on to state that telecommuters are
"normal" employees, work on a volunteer basis, and
spend only a portion of their work time at home. It
also boasts that this type of work is especially successful with the more highly qualified employees.
One fact that did seem to escape American companies and one which became a cornerstone for the
Netherlands experiment is that for the program to be
successful the practitioner must spend a minimum
of one-fifth of his time at home. Less than this and

the worker's efforts were actually set back instead of enhanced.

Addressing the question of supervisory personnel, the Netherlands study concluded that, in reality, many managers when asked the whereabouts of their employees were unable to say precisely where they were. Because of business trips, meetings, conferences with other employees, and movement within the office building, it is entirely possible for a worker to be away from his or her desk for hours at a time. This being the case, the study concludes, why worry about the insignificant things? As long as an employee is productive, it doesn't matter if his work is done from his desk, his home, or the executive wash room. In a large organization, idling behind a desk is relatively easy. In telecommuting, one is forced to show real production. And production was up at the Hauge by 25 percent!

In a survey taken after the initial nine month experiment was over, 80 percent of the participants felt that their production was up, their job satisfaction level was considerably higher, and their attitude toward their job was greatly increased. Their reasons for this sudden appreciation for their jobs were as varied as the jobs they did. One worker cited the fact that he no longer had to put up with smokers in his office environment. Another cited the fact that he didn't have as many interruptions from his colleagues whom he claimed wasted a goodly amount of his day in their efforts to look busy. One person even claimed that working at home allowed her child to understand better what it was that her mother did each day and how important her work was. Almost to the person, however, what they liked best was the fact that on days they telecommuted, they didn't have to drive into the city.

The RIV concluded that if other departments wanted to telecommute, they would do well to remember six points.

1)  Establish a procedure, and then follow it. Do not change the plan every Monday morning. Consistency, while it may well be the hobgoblin of little minds, is also the central post upon which to hang telecommuting habits and policies.

2)  Be cautious when purchasing hardware and software for use in the telecommuting program. They warn potential managers that often the companies which market these goods will have a tendency to overstate the capabilities of their product while downplaying the degree of difficulty the average worker will encounter learning to use the new programs.

3)  Take care to see that the proper number of data lines and telephone lines are installed before the program gets off the ground. Also, check the scheduling of when these lines will be available, and as important, when they will not.

4)  See that all personnel involved in the plan are consulted on a regular basis. Never let an employee get too far away from the control of the office. *Every remote control device has a limit as to its range.* Long distance

management is no different. There is a difference between remote control and no control!

5) Be careful to stay one step ahead of technology. It would be very simple to fall behind in the world of high-tech, especially when the workers are not always present in the office to discuss the latest advancements in technology. It becomes that much more critical when the person responsible for office machine procurement is at home telecommuting.

6) Start small. Don't send the entire office staff home from the start. Begin with a few of the better workers and slowly involve others who wish to try home working. There are two reasons for this. First, it is easier to monitor a handful of workers in the beginning. Remember, this is new to the supervisor as well as the home worker. Secondly, if the plan doesn't work out, there is considerable less trouble in dismantling the program if there are fewer workers involved.

# Epilogue

There is no doubt telecommuting is the wave of the future, and there is no doubt that when it becomes common practice, it will do so with a speed that will make lightning look slow. The technology necessary for this concept is already in place. The need is clearly present. All that remains to be done in order for telecommuting to become a full-fledged employment practice is the breaking down of barriers which many managers have erected to protect what they perceive to be a threat to their future.

There are two ways to deal with the facts of economic life that telecommuting will offer. First, a company can fight the trend, refuse to recognize the inevitability of this alternative course of commerce, and enter the next decade and the next century of American business scratching and fighting all the way. The second choice is to accept and capitalize on what is surely the greatest change in life and work styles this country has seen since the industrial revolution! If companies can see the handwriting on the wall and, more importantly, read that handwriting, they will lead their industries into the twenty-first century.

The company that choses to embrace telecommuting will be the company that out produces, out hires, and out sells its competitors. The choice is yours. Lead or follow. Remember, Ford was the *first* real innovative automobile manufacturer in America. Hudson was the *second*. Has anyone driven a Hudson lately?

# Glossary of Terms

**Access Code**   That code Which must be given in response to a computer system inquiry, which establishes the identity of the user. This may be either numeric or alpha in origin, and in very sophisticated systems, may even be something as personal as finger, hand, or voice imprints.

**Cottage Industry**   Any industrial function which can be performed in the home, or any portion thereof, such as glove manufacturing, or the sewing of buttons on garments. Other cottage industries include jewelry manufacture, envelope stuffing, fishing lure construction, etc.

**Employment Characteristic Analysis**   A set of questions which will aid the employer in his determination of whether or not a particular employee will be able to conform to the unusual requirements of telecommuting.

**FSLA**   Fair Labor Standards Act of 1938 passed in response to Labor Union pressure. It outlawed seven home cottage industries, primarily concerning garment and glove manufacturing.

**Global commodity**   Any product or service which transcends geographic borders and which can be produced or serviced without regard to borders or language barriers.

**Growth Adjustments**   Those periods of time when the expansion of a corporate endeavor cause a temporary slow down in production, due solely to the lack of facilities or personnel.

**Independent Contractors**   Those workers who remain outside the mainstream of an organization, while performing specified jobs for specific periods of time for pre-agreed upon rates, either piece meal, or by the job. In most cases, but certainly not all, the independent contractor works outside the physical business offices of the contract provider.

**Iron Collar Workers**    reference robotics

**Manage by Activity**   The inclination to measure success based solely on activity on the part of the employee.

**Manage by Productivity**   The inclination of measure success based solely on production and quotas.

**Modems**   That device, which when connected to a computer system, gives the computer system the capability of communication with other systems, through the use of telephone or satellite hookups.

**Off-sight office**     see satellite office.

**Off-sight workers**     People working away from the main office of a company.

**Perimeter Audio Device**     An alarm system which is designed to protect a specified area, usually a single room, and generally works on a laser or motion detector basis.

**Pink Collar Workers**     reference to female employees

**Satellite Office**     Any office that exists primarily as a work center for the employees stationed there, but not as corporate headquarters. Such offices serve to focus the central gathering of related or unrelated corporate employees.

**Telecommuting**     The act of employment by which an employee performs his or her duties from a remote location, on a regular basis, and sends the production of that employment to the central or home office via modem, fax, or currier.

**Telecommuting Work Stations**     All things which go into the establishment and management of a home or satellite work area. This usually consists of all furniture, hardware, computers, faxes, modems, phones, phone lines, electrical connections, and office supplies.

**Teleconference**   The gathering of three or more people for the purpose of conducting business, and that gathering being done by a single phone call during which all concerned parties are present via phone lines.

**Time Frame**   The amount of time allocated to the completion of a certain aspect of an overall project.

**Time Lines**   A means of measurement to determine whether or not a particular project is on schedule, and to chart the progress thereof.

**Time Tables**   The overall amount of time allocated to any single or specified project.

**Transparency**   The degree to which any telecommuting project can be accomplished without outsiders being aware of the fact that certain employees are operating outside the traditional role of office workers.

**Work-o-tels**   The European counterpart to the U.S. concept of the satellite offices. The main point of Work-o-tels is that they are often shared between several companies, not just workers within the same company.

# Index

**A**

AFL-CIO, 171–173
Alarms, 113–114
Ambassador College/Swift-
    Net Project, 143–146
Americans with Disabili-
    ties Act of 1991,
    165–166
  *See* Hiring
Assignment. *See* Produc-
    tion
AT&T, 145
Attitudinal. *See* Pre-pilot

**B**

Bank and Bank Revision
    Act (1980), 187
Benefits

differences, 50
employee, 18
fringe, 151
health, 6
life, 6
payroll, 104
shared, 24
social/personal, 28
telecommuting, 74–75
Bureau of Labor Statis-
    tics, 172
Business activities, 107–
    108

**C**

California Western Life
    (Cal-West), 151–155,
    160
Clerical workers, 57

Committee on Govern-
   ment Operations, 166
Communication skills,
   33–35
Common Market, 188
Commuting, 19
  See Telecommuting
  cost, 20
  foreign oil, reduction,
   27–28
  mass transit, 25–26
Compensation, 74–75, 152
Competition
  increasing, 182–183
  world economy, factors,
   182–185
Computer, 41
  technology, 110–112
Contact, 66
Contract, 76–77
Contractor, independent,
   105–107, 109
Coolidge, Calvin, 4
Corporations. See Private
   corporations
Cottage industry, 23
Crane and Associates,
   149–151

D

Data
  entry, 9, 41
  lines, 5
  management depart-
   ment, 86
  Processing Department,
   94
  security, 110

Department of Labor
  State of California, 44
  United States, 42
Department of Public
   Works (DPW), 121
Deregulation, 183
Desk terminals, 6
Disasters, natural, 17
Divorce, 22

E

Economy
  See Competition
  global, 179–181
  world, factors of competition, 182–185
EDP System Analysts, 121
E-Mail, 5, 33, 95
Employee
  See Savings
  Benefits Department, 94
  Characteristic Assess-
   ment, 123–126
   survey, 124–126
  characteristics, 125–126
  corporate, 22–24
  retention, 150
  Telecommuting Survey,
   136–142
Employment and Housing
   subcommittee, 166–
   167
Environmental impact,
   16–17
  reduced pollution, 24–25
Expenses
  unnecessary, 13–14
Experience. See Job

**F**

Fair Labor Standards Act
of 1938 (FLSA), 170
Fax machines, 6, 33, 47,
61, 93, 103
Federal statutes, 166–168
Feedback, 156
Flexibility, 84–85
Ford Motor Company, 96

**G**

Global implications, 179–
193
Glossary, 197–200
Goals
establishing, 67–68
reasonable, 85
Government entities, 119–
146
corporations' compli-
ance, 165–175

**H**

Handicapped. *See* Ameri-
cans, Hiring
Harvard School of Busi-
ness, 45
Hiring
*See* Americans, Em-
ployee, Job, Recruit-
ment
handicapped, 14–15
telecommuters, 156
Home office. *See* Office

**I**

Implications. *See* Global
implications
Insurance, 101
International Ladies
Garment Workers
Union (ILGWU), 174
Inter-office memos, 33

**J**

Job
expectations, 47–50
experience, 32–33

**L**

Labor pool, 7
increasing, 15–16
Land Surveyor, assistant,
121
Legislative compliance,
165–175
Liability
employee, 100–102
factors
telecommuting, 99–116
product, 99–100
property, 102–104
security, 109–113
tax, 104–109

**M**

Mainframe equipment, 61
Managed Care Depart-
ment, 94

Management's survey,
   132–136
Managers
   *See* Job, Telecommuting
   characteristics, 131–132
   guidelines, 81–86
   objectives, 10
   profile, 45–47
   telecommuting adjust-
      ment, 41–43, 44–45
   trust, 48
Managing
   telecommuter, 65–72
Mass transit. *See* Com-
   muting
Meetings, 34
Megatek Industries, 158–
   162
Ministry of Social Affairs,
   190
Ministry of Transport for
   Netherlands (RIV),
   189–191
Modem, 6, 41, 61
Monitoring
   telecommuter, 65–77,
   122
Morale, 121
Motivating
   telecommuter, 65–77
Moving, planning, 54–59

**N**

National Association of
   Dry Cleaners, 20

**O**

Objectives, 82–83
Office
   *See* Regimen, Schedule
   home
      comfort, 38–40
      organizing, 36–37
      returning, 75–76
      traditional, 10–13, 172
Organization, 35–36, 82–
   83
Organized labor, 170–175

**P**

Pacific Bell, 95
Perks, 104
Personnel
   *See* Communication,
      Hiring, Job experience
   finding, 31–50
Plan. *See* Telecommuting
Pollution. *See* Environ-
   mental impact
Pool. *See* Labor pool
Pre-pilot attitudinal sur-
   vey, 123, 132–136
Printouts, 115
Private corporations
   telecommuting, 149–162
   aiding government
compliance, 165–175
Privatization, 184
Production, assignment,
   66–67

Productivity
  increased/ing, 18–20,
    55, 58, 121
  loss, 53
Promotion, 157
Proposition 111, 120
Protectionism, 186–187

**R**

Recruitment
  See Employee, Hiring
  procedures, 89–92
Regimen, establishing, 40–
    41
Regulations, 72
Retirement, 6
RIV. See Ministry of
  Transport
Rules, 72

**S**

Sales
  clerk, 88
  conversion to
telecommuting, 57–58
  manager, 58
  orders, 9
  retail, 181
San Diego County
  Telecommuting
  Project, 119–143
  results, 142–143
  surveys, 124–126, 127–
    132, 133–136, 137–
    142
Savings, tangible, 20–21

Schedule
  See Timetable
  establishing, 37–38
Scientific Application Inc.
  (S.A.I.), 161
Screening process, 123
Security, 26–27
  See Liability
  increasing, 113–116
Self-starters, 32, 123
Semi-Public entities
  telecommuting, 119–146
Service industries (U.S.),
    185–188
Service Employees Union
  (SEU), 173
Skills. See Communication
Staff, in-house, 83–84
Software, 61, 158
Supervisors, 32, 123
  Screening Survey, 127–
    132
SwiftNet. See Ambassador

**T**

Tariffs, 184
Taxation, 13–14
  See Liability, United
States
  ad valorem, 13–14
  property, 14
Team spirit, 84
Telecommunication
  See Job
  categories, 3
  contact, 48–49
  environment, adapta-
    tion, 41–43

faith, 82
history, 4–8
introduction, 3–28
program, implementa-
    tion, 53–61
trust, 48
Telecommuting
  See Commuting, Govern-
    ment, Manager, Semi-
    Public
  corporations. See Pri-
    vate corporations
  definition, 56
  experiments in Europe,
    189–193
  implementation, 59–61,
    92–96, 100, 154
  implications. See Global
    levels, 155
  liability factors. See Lia-
    bility perimeters,
    setting, 81–96
  plan, 87–89
  preparation, 72–74
  program
    beginning, 53–62
    cost, 55
    setting up, 122–123
  project factors, 61–62,
    86–87
  screening, 123, 127–132
  Survey for Employees,
    See Employees
  time, 86–87
Teleconferences, 83
Telex lines, 5

Terminals, 61, 102, 114
Time frames, 70–71
Timelines, 71–72
Timetables
  See Schedule
  establishing, 67–70
  factors, 86–87
Travelers Company, 9,
    32, 56, 93–94, 155–
    158

U

United Parcel Service, 43,
    58
United States Tax Code,
    168–169

V

Video display screens, 114
Voice mail, 5, 33, 95

W

WATS lines, 6
Work
  characteristics, 126, 131
  hours, change, 72–74
  off-site worker, 35, 91
  week, 19
  work-at-home, 167
World War II, 7
World Wide Church of
    God, 143